Type from the Desktop

Designing with Type and Your Computer

Type from the Desktop: Designing with Type and Your Computer
Copyright © 1990 Clifford Burke

Library of Congress Cataloging-in-Publication Data

Burke, Clifford, 1942-
    Type from the desktop: designing with type and your computer
/ by Clifford Burke. — 1st ed.
                    p.   cm.
    Includes bibliographical references.
    ISBN 0-940087-45-6
    1. Desktop publishing—Style manuals. 2. Printing,
Practical—Layout—Data processing. 3. Computerized typesetting.
I. Title.
Z286.D47B83 1990
686.2'2544536—dc20   90-12203
                    CIP

Cover design: Patrick Short, Dancing Bear Graphics, Raleigh, NC
Desktop publishing and illustrations: Cassell Design, Durham, NC
Linotronic output: Azalea Typography, Durham, NC
Art director: Karen Wysocki, Ventana Press
Technical editor: David Lemon, Berkeley, CA
Editorial staff: Marion Laird, Terry Patrickis, Jeff Qualls, Elizabeth Shoemaker, Sarah Wadsworth

Portions of Chapter 6 were previously published in *Publish!*, 501 Second Street, San Francisco, CA 94107.

For Information about our audio products, write us at:
First Edition, First Printing   Newbridge Book Clubs, 3000 Cindel Drive, Delran, NJ 08370
Printed in the United States of America

Ventana Press, Inc.
P.O. Box 2468
Chapel Hill, NC 27515
919/942-0220
919/942-1140 Fax

Limits of Liability and Disclaimer

The author and publisher have used their best efforts in preparing this book. The author and publisher make no warranty of any kind, expressed or implied, with regard to the instructions and suggestions contained in this book.

About the Author

Clifford Burke is a poet, a former traditional letterpress printer and publisher (during the small-press renaissance of the Sixties and Seventies in San Francisco), and a freelance writer and book designer. He is the author of *Printing It* and *Printing Poetry*, two previous books on printing and typography; five volumes of poetry; and two travel guides to his native Pacific Northwest. As a contributing editor to *Publish!* Magazine, he writes the monthly "About Faces" column on typeface design and history.

Acknowledgments

I would like to thank the following folks for their unique contributions along the way of this book:

Dawn Ashbach, Garrett Boge, Liz Bond, Fred Brady, Ernie Brock, Margery Cantor, Robin Casady, Keith Cassell, Mary Cochran, Tom Conroy, Barbara Evans Cram, Louise Dominitz, Earl Douglas, Dal Farias, Jim Felici, Peter Fraterdeus, Bo Galford, Gerald Giampa, Susan Gubernat, Delphine Haley, Glen Hughes, Lilly Kaufman, Randall Kincaid, David Lemon, Jeff Level, Cheryl Miller, Joseph Miller & Family, Virginia Mudd, Roger C. Parker, Tom Pickett, Will Powers, David Slabaugh, Henry Schneiker, Judith Sutcliffe, Susan Tweit, Becky Walker, Jake Widman, Judith Winter, Karen Wysocki and, of course, my family: Fenicia, Clea and Margaret Burke.

This book is dedicated to my brothers, Dan and Steve.

Trademarks

Table of Contents

Introduction   xv

1   Getting Started   1

What Is Type?   1

What Is Typography?   3

Type and Visual Communication   3

Typeface Design   4

White Space   5

Did I Mention Fun?   6

Concept and Context   6

What Comes First?   6

The Design Process: Thinking It Through   7

A Business Letter Is Not a Newsletter   8

Scope   9

Audience   9

The Format   9

Structure   9

Production   10

The Dynamic of Black and White   10

Editorial Work   12

2 Setting Up Your Text 17

Setting Margins 18

Margin Size 19

Margins and Columns 21

Margins and Facing Pages 23

Exploring New Territory 24

White Space 25

Line Length and Type Size 25

Line Length 26

Type Size 27

Letter Shapes and Proportions 28

Line Spacing 29

Alignment 30

Justification 30

Flush-Left/Ragged-Right 33

Formality and Informality

Flush-Right/Ragged-Left 36

Word Spacing 36

Letter Spacing—Tracking and Kerning 38

Tracking 38

Kerning 40

Spacing Around Those Pesky Points and Figures 41

3 Choosing a Typeface 45

What Is a Typeface? 46

Serif Type 47

Sans-Serif Type 48

A Thumbnail History of Type 49

Old Style 50

Transitional Designs 52

Modern 52

Slab Serifs   54

Old Style Revivals   55

Emergence of Sans-Serif Type   56

Contemporary   57

Allusive Typography   58

Some Faces Do Everything   59

4   Adding Display Type   63

Display Face Options   64

Uppercase Text Font   64

Italic Text Font   64

Text Font Size   65

Boldface Text Font   66

Spacing Display Type   66

Alignment of Heads   68

Flush-Left; Ragged-Left and Mixed;
Centered Headings; Letter-Spaced Capitals;
Kerning

Mixing Typefaces   75

Some Rules of Thumb for Combining Typefaces   76

Sizing Display Type   80

How Big, How Small?   80

Relationships; Consistency

Pull-Quotes and Sidebars   82

5   Type as Ornamentation   87

Decorative Letters   87

Manipulation Effects   89

Type Families   89

Ornamental Faces   90

Dingbats   93

Other Graphic Devices   94

 How Much Is Too Much?   96

 Runarounds   98

 Reverses   99

 Special Type Characters   100

6   Building Your Type Library   103

Augmenting Resident Fonts   104

Text Faces Form the Core   105

Which Supplier? Which Versions?   107

Type Organizer   109

 Historical   110

  Bembo; Garamond; Janson; Galliard/Granjon; Caslon;

  Baskerville; Bodoni; Clarendons/Slab Serif; Italics

 Decorative   128

  Blackletter; Uncial; Script; Poster

 The Types of Frederic W. Goudy   132

 Resident Fonts   134

  Times; Helvetica; Palatino

 Contemporary   140

  The Stone Family

 Sans-Serif   142

  Gill Sans; Futura; Optima

How to Look at Typefaces   148

7   Design Considerations   155

 Logical Flow / Continuity   156

 Balance / Dynamic Harmony   157

 Simplicity   158

 Consistency   159

 Involvement   160

8 Creating Your Design and Layout   163

What Is It?   163

Who Will Read It?   164

What Should It Look Like?   164

How Big Should It Be?   166

First Steps   167

Making It Happen: Conceptualization   168

The Thumbnail Sketch   168

The Dummy   169

Trial Proofs   170

Two Approaches to the Layout   172

Grids   172

Organic Layout   173

Letting Form Follow Function   175

9 Production   179

Know Your Tools   179

Service Bureaus   182

Talking to Real Printers   182

Other Expert Help   184

Selecting Paper   184

Paper Conservation & Recycling   187

10 Money, Time & Fun   191

Money   191

Time   192

Fun   193

Glossary   195

Bibliography 203

Type Makers 207

Typefaces Mentioned 209

Type Specifications for This Book 211

Index 213

Introduction

You see it again and again—the ubiquitous Helvetica/Times Roman typeface combo. As if it were stamped or branded, you know at a glance that the document you're reading originated on a desktop publishing system. And you wonder, Is there more to desktop publishing than this?

The answer is yes. The world of typography, once the domain of a few master craftsmen, is now accessible to everyone involved with electronic publishing. And it can take you far beyond Helvetica and Times Roman.

Rich in variety and aesthetics, steeped in tradition yet vital and contemporary, type is the cornerstone of print communications and design. It shapes, enhances and enlivens what we have to say on the page.

In short, yes there *is* a lot more to desktop publishing than those overused typefaces, although they too have a legitimate place in a desktop typographer's collection. And as you explore the wealth of choices, you'll realize that each typeface and type style has a language all its own, molded by history and designed to project a special tone or feeling.

Who Should Read This Book?

Type from the Desktop is a generic guide for anyone who produces documents, presentations or other forms of printed material with any electronic publishing system. It's designed to help you use your nascent abilities to handle, assemble and present information more effectively, whether it be in print or on screen.

This book will help you make informed choices about typography, regardless of your level of design expertise. Even if you're using a page layout program for the first time, *Type from the Desktop* should enable you to understand typographic and design principles while you're actually producing pages.

How to Use This Book

There's a hierarchy to typographic construction that generally follows the procedures adopted by most desktop publishing software. This book is structured to reflect that sequence.

The first chapter offers an overall introduction to type and typography, its many uses and levels of meaning. It also addresses preliminary practical matters, such as defining the scope of your project, the importance of having finished files to work with and knowing who your readers are.

The next four chapters cover formats and type choices for all elements of printed work—from text to display type. You'll learn about the subtle but important nuances of line and letter spacing, type size, columns, decorative type and graphics. In addition, the fascinating history of type and its influence on today's choices are explored.

Chapter 6 is devoted to in-depth examinations of various typefaces and type combinations. Typeface selections begin with those most commonly found on desktop printers and move on to include important historical models available from contemporary digital font manufacturers. Typeface structure is discussed and new designs in the digital medium are also featured.

The remaining chapters cover design principles, layout and production, including organic layout, thumbnail sketches, "dummy" pages and trial proofs.

Type from the Desktop was written to help you find your working and learning level and go on from there. You'll quickly realize the powerful effect that type choices have on a printed page and the joys of matching the time-honored craft of typography with the technological advances of electronic publishing.

Clifford Burke
Anacortes, Washington

CHAPTER ONE

Getting Started

Getting Started

When you first took up the tools of this young sport we call Desktop Publishing, you entered a community finding its way among conventions hundreds of years old, yet constantly being reshaped by fresh discoveries. Technology has opened the door to an exciting, accessible new method of personal publishing, combining the venerable traditions of printing and typography with the speed and convenience of computer automation. Even we old-timers are new at it.

As you learn the tools of desktop publishing and perhaps discover your own hidden design abilities, you'll recognize how essential typography really is. For the setting up and arranging of type are at the very foundation of publishing, both in its traditional forms and on the desktop.

What Is Type?

Type is the published form of writing. Private writing—the handwritten letter you send to your best pal—is deliberately informal and intimate, and you wouldn't want it any other way. But when you're writing something to be read by a stranger, or by more than one person, then your message is better delivered through the formality and legibility of type. Except perhaps for graffiti, where the typography is spontaneous and direct, the letters we see in print were created through a mechanical process to make them as readable as possible to a large number of people.

So type is really just the mechanical version of handwriting—formal, public and endlessly reproducible.

What makes type fun, but sometimes frustrating, is that since its invention several centuries ago, hundreds of different "typefaces," or styles, have been created—at different times and places—to suit various needs and visions. Many of these styles have been resurrected or reinterpreted in digital form for desktop publishing. This accumulated history, now alive and well in small computers and laser printers everywhere, makes an incredibly rich resource for designing publications. It also offers a fertile area of exploration and discovery for anybody willing to pursue it.

What Is Typography?

The study of typefaces, and how to use them, is called typography. Just by looking at the myriad styles of type, it's easy to see that typog-

raphy as a study can be very deep and complex. Yet, as a craft, it can be a simple and straightforward matter of good judgment and taste.

One of the things I like best about type is that it belongs to everybody. Not all of us are artists, illustrators, graphic designers or professional typographers—thank goodness. But we all grow up with an intuitive sense of type's functions, just from our constant exposure to it.

Typography is the craft and skill of arranging letters and words—working out logical order, priorities, sequences and placement. In this respect, typography is somewhat like editing.

Typography is also an art. Aesthetic intuition, combined with knowledge of materials and skill with tools, makes typography work. Although there's nothing particularly esoteric about typography, it must be learned, like any other art or craft.

Type and Visual Communication

Another level of typographic skill goes beyond the fundamentals and into the broad, historically rich world of typographic design: the subtleties of manipulating type can make words sing (and even dance) on the page and shape objects of beauty out of language and the presentation of language. Making things happen visually on a page is one of the great rewards of working with type.

With the proliferation of desktop publishing, typographic design is no longer the sole province of specialists. Today, the only limitations are your level of interest and application in pursuing this skill.

Typeface Design

The printed alphabet's commonality of shapes makes it at least a logical realm. On one hand, modern typefaces aren't too different in structure from the ancient ones. Throughout their long history, the letters of the roman alphabet have remained consistently recognizable. The letter A, for example, found its original form in early biblical times and has never lost its identity. So when you enter typography, you're on pretty firm historical ground. You can trust your senses to tell you that an A is an A.

On the other hand, the number of alphabet design variations is enormous. With this vast array of typefaces at your disposal, here's where typography comes into play. While similarity among typeface characters is obvious, the many available interpretations can accommodate a wide range of expression.

Simply put, your typeset pages will express something different set in a typeface invented in the 17th century than in a typeface designed by Hermann Zapf in the 1950s or one designed specifically for laser printers. Likewise, headings set in a big, scrunched-up, blocky face will convey something different from heads set in a frilly copperplate script. Perhaps typefaces are called faces because they have personalities and, like human faces, show their history and sensibilities.

"This country, with its institutions, belongs to the people who inhabit it.
Whenever they shall grow weary of the existing government, they can exercise their constitutional right of amending it, or their constitutional right to dismember or overthrow it."

Abraham Lincoln

Janson

"This country, with its institutions, belongs to the people who inhabit it.
Whenever they shall grow weary of the existing government, they can exercise their constitutional right of amending it, or their constitutional right to dismember or overthrow it."

Abraham Lincoln

Stone Serif

Once you begin to see how it's possible to express yourself in the way words look as well as in what they say, you're on your way toward good typography. Variations within typeface "families," as well as the range in shape, size, "personality" and historical association, make it possible to achieve good design with nothing but type alone—with good judgment rather than a talent for drawing and illustration.

White Space

A very important element in typography is space—black letters and white space. The real stuff of good typography is in the way you manipulate space on the two-dimensional page, how you arrange typefaces within the space, and how you connect type and space logically and consistently to make a readable, whole thing.

Along the way, you should learn when to call on the help of design and printing professionals. Graphic arts specialists acquire expertise through long training and experience. Knowing when you have a problem beyond your abilities is a primary learning goal at this level.

Getting the Output You Want

The printed alphabet's commonality of shapes makes it at least a logical realm. On one hand, modern typefaces aren't too different in structure from the ancient ones. Throughout their long history, the letters of the roman alphabet have remained consistently recognizable. The letter A, for example, found its original form in early biblical times and has never lost its identity. So when you enter typography, you're on pretty firm historical ground. You can trust your senses to tell you that an A is an A.

On the other hand, the number of alphabet design variations is enormous. With this vast array of typefaces at your disposal, here's where typography comes into play. While similarity among typeface characters is obvious, the many available interpretations can accommodate a wide range of expression.

Simply put, your typeset pages will express something different set in a typeface invented in the 17th century than in a typeface designed by Hermann Zapf in the 1950s or one designed specifically for laser printers. Likewise, headings set in a big, scrunched-up, blocky face will convey something different from heads set in a frilly copperplate script. Perhaps typefaces are called faces because they have personalities and, like human faces, show their history and sensibilities.

Once you begin to see how it's possible to express yourself in the way words look as well as in what they say, you're on your way toward good typography. Variations within typeface "families," as well as the range in shape, size, "personality" and historical association, make it possible to achieve good design with nothing but type alone—with good judgment rather than a talent for drawing and illustration.

A very important element in typography is space—black letters and white space. The real stuff of good typography is in the way you manipulate space on the two-dimen-

Getting the Output You Want

The printed alphabet's commonality of shapes makes it at least a logical realm. On one hand, modern typefaces aren't too different in structure from the ancient ones. Throughout their long history, the letters of the roman alphabet have remained consistently recognizable. The letter A, for example, found its original form in early biblical times and has never lost its identity. So when you enter typography, you're on pretty firm historical ground. You can trust your senses to tell you that an A is an A.

On the other hand, the number of alphabet design variations is enormous. With this vast array of typefaces at your disposal, here's where typography comes into play. While similarity among typeface characters is obvious, the many available interpretations can accommodate a wide range of expression.

White space used effectively can transform gray, dense pages into well-designed, inviting ones.

Did I Mention Fun?

I have found typography to be a rewarding pursuit for a quarter of a century (!) and in many ways it's just as much fun in digital form as it was in the old days of lead. It's a demanding craft, and often frustrating. But language is in us all, and it's very satisfying to watch a latent ability for composition play itself out to the fullest on the computer screen. Just wait till you gain a little proficiency with your page layout program and learn to recognize a handful of companionable typefaces. As you find yourself winging through subtleties of sizes, combinations and placement, you'll begin to see how this kind of effective and useful play can be fascinating for a lifetime.

Concept and Context

Before plunging into the chapters on setting up pages, a few basic concepts will help speed you on your way.

What Comes First?

Basic layout decisions related to image and space, margins, line length and space between them are not totally dependent on typeface selection. In fact, the typeface choice for any part of a job (e.g., text or titles) can be made simultaneously with many other design decisions. And typeface design is rarely critical to those decisions. So, for the purposes of getting started, it doesn't matter which typeface you choose.

For now, get acquainted with all the faces you have available by setting trial pages and experimenting as often as time and inclination allow. Learn to recognize their appearance on the screen and resulting effects on the printed page. And focus on some of the more immediate considerations, such as content, purpose and overall structure.

N ear its core, typography is a thinking process. It's not a particularly difficult one. It's fun. And it's the key to good-looking pages and effective publications. You might think of this part of your work as "design." True design lies not in the clever image, but in the logical structure—something that rarely wins awards, but makes your readers appreciate your efforts ~~without even knowing it.~~

N ear its core, typography is a thinking process. It's not a particularly difficult one. It's fun. And it's the key to good-looking pages and effective publications. You might think of this part of your work as "design." True design lies not in the clever image, but in the logical structure—something that rarely wins awards, but makes your readers appreciate your efforts without ~~even knowing~~ it. If a ~~printed~~

The Design Process: Thinking It Through

At its core, typography is a thinking process. It's not a particularly difficult one. It's fun. And it's the key to good-looking pages and effective publications. You might think of this part of your work as "design."

True design lies not in the clever image, but in the logical structure—something that rarely wins awards, but makes your readers appreciate your efforts without even knowing it. If a printed piece is clear, you have won most of the battles for the reader's attention and involvement.

A Business Letter Is Not a Newsletter

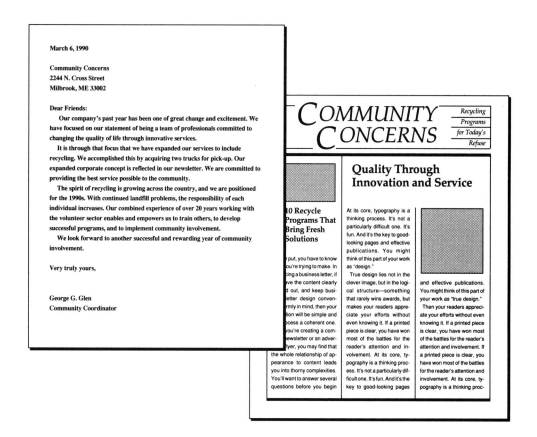

Simply put, you have to know what you're trying to make. In producing a business letter, if you have the content clearly worked out, and keep business letter design conventions firmly in mind, then your projection will be simple and the process a coherent one.

But if you're creating a company newsletter or an advertising flyer, you may find that the whole relationship of appearance to content leads you into thorny complexities. You'll want to answer several questions before you begin trying to position a miscellaneous handful of articles and graphics or other items.

The process of "thinking it through" goes something like this:

Scope

Another way to look at the scope of a project is to ask yourself, How big is it? This does not merely relate to format but has more to do with the extent of the idea. Think of the number of political candidates who have lost their campaign because they had to put their entire political philosophy on a promo piece, which nobody bothered to read. Defining the scope of a project is an editorial process as well and must be done in conjunction with the preparation of the text.

Audience

One of my teachers said, you don't set the menu in tiny script type for a luncheon honoring octogenarians; you don't print a concert program on paper that crackles. This is the best description I know of design, what it is and what it ain't. Think about who you're trying to reach. If the answer is obvious, you can plan accordingly. If the answer is not so apparent, then part of your design work is to develop the potential audience in the way the material is presented. Sears Catalog readers aren't the same as Banana Republic shoppers, generally speaking.

The Format

The choice of format—shape and size—is often predetermined by available production facilities (such as a laser printer) or by the conventions of the kind of piece you're doing (e.g., a business letter). Some concepts cry out for unusual formats, and page layout programs are flexible in their ability to display unusual shapes. Keep in mind, however, that your printer, or any printer, may not be able to handle the thing you think up. Don't forget production.

Structure

A piece carefully edited before publishing will have the contents' levels of importance worked out. And in some cases, as in a letter, the structure of the contents is clear. But where the contents are diverse, or typographic elements are key to clarity of presentation, it's important to work out conceptually the way the publication will lead from the important material through to the less important in a logical and reader-friendly way.

Production

A thousand newsletters are not produced the same way as ten copies of a memo to associates. However, for the purposes of typography, what really matters most is the way in which the prepared pages enter the production process—either as xerographic copies from your laser printer or as photographic output from a service bureau—and the decision is often based on the typefaces you have available in your own system.

What you've probably noticed, and will see again throughout this book, is that design elements are interlocking. Typeface, size and spacing all work in relation to one another. Scope, format and production process must be worked out referentially, since one aspect of a design may have profound effects on another area you thought you'd already worked out.

But that's part of the fun of it, to make these puzzle pieces called letters, words, paragraphs, columns and pages all fit together and knock the socks off some bored client.

The Dynamic of Black and White

The dynamic balancing of image and space works on the many levels of a publication to create visual interest, readable texts and appropriate design. Whatever the color of your dreams, or the kaleidoscopic intricacy of the printed pieces you create on your desktop system, it's important to keep in mind that the fundamentals of typography are worked out in black and white—or, if you prefer, positive image and negative space—whatever the actual colors may be.

One of the most useful skills you can develop in desktop publishing is learning to see the shapes of white spaces in and around the pages you're working on. There's a kind of hierarchy of relationships between black and white that should be kept in mind, and typographic construction should reflect this structure.

Getting the Output You Want

The dynamic balancing of image and space works on the many levels of a publication to create visual interest, readable texts and appropriate design. Whatever the color of your dreams, or the kaleidoscopic intricacy of the printed pieces you create on your desktop system, it's important to keep in mind that the fundamentals of typography are worked out in black and white—or, if you prefer, positive image and negative space—whatever the actual colors may be.

One of the most useful skills you can develop in desktop publishing is learning to see the shapes of white spaces in and around the pages you're working on. There's a kind of hierarchy of relationships between black and white that should be kept in mind, and typographic construction should reflect this structure.The dynamic balancing of image and space works on the many levels of a publication to create visual interest, readable texts and appropri-

But that's part of the fun of it, to make these puzzle pieces called letters, words, paragraphs, columns and pages all fit together and knock the socks off some bored client.

ate design. Whatever the color of your dreams, or the kaleidoscopic intricacy of the printed pieces you create on your desktop system, it's important to keep in mind that the fundamentals of typography are worked out in black and white—or, if you prefer, positive image and negative space— whatever the actual colors may be. One of the most useful skills you can develop in desktop publishing is learning to see the shapes of white spaces in and around the pages you're working on. There's a kind of hierarchy of relationships between black and white that should be kept in mind, and typographic construction should reflect this structure. One of the most useful skills you can develop in desktop publishing is learning to see.

The following are the levels at which typography should enhance the reading process.

▶ The overall image block on the page or "spread" (facing pages in a book or report).

▶ The relationship between columns (e.g., a newsletter).

▶ The effect of the spacing between lines and between words.

▶ The subtle dynamic of the space within and around the letters themselves.

▶ The shapes of the typeface characters and how they fit together.

To look at the balance of black and white at any of these levels, to appreciate the dynamic involved, it helps to see the context without the content—in other words, to see the shapes involved without

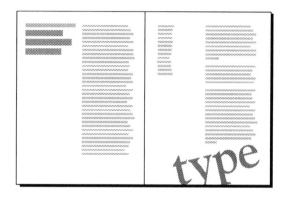

reading the words. To do this, I use a technique called "squinting." Since the first bear painting on a cave wall, artisans have been stepping back to size up the visual objects their hands have made, the way my granddad used to step back and squint at a line of masonry or a boatwright eyes a fair curve. Squinting produces an altered visual perception of the problem, revealing dynamic relationships rather than details of component parts.

One of the things I like about working on the computer screen is that it gives you a small-scale, rough rendition of the page. What you see is not the contents or even specific typefaces, but rather the thing in miniature. In desktop publishing, you have a built-in squinting device.

Editorial Work

Before you delve into typography, it's important to think about the actual material you'll be working with.

There's a strong temptation to pick out a typeface and get rolling. But if you rush along too quickly, you'll end up having to make complicated adjustments late in the assembly process. Although some programs are more cooperative with late changes than others, it's a minor myth that electronic changes are quick and simple to make right up to the last minute, as you're firing pages off to the printer. The biggest problem is that one small change can affect your entire layout structure. So it's important that your raw material, the digital information you'll manipulate within your page layout program, be complete.

Whenever a manuscript is prepared for printing, it follows a style established for the treatment of literary conventions, spelling, punctuation and to some extent the handling of the language. Editors call this a "house style," which isn't the same as style in design or styles of type. House style assures that all the contents of a work are consistent and perhaps conform to a larger series of publications. If there is no method in your work for establishing this kind of editorial consistency, it would be good to create one. A standard reference work on publication style is *The Chicago Manual of Style*, published by the University of Chicago Press.

If you are new to the computerized word-assembly environment, it will serve you well to stop and consider the implications of the way computers handle words. Imagine word processing as a continuous text string—a line of letters, punctuation, spaces and symbols. Carriage returns, paragraph indents, page breaks and margins—known as page setup in most word-handling software—are all things you must create as separate functions.

What used to be delivered to the printer was a manuscript marked up for editorial changes, typographic style and design specifications. The printer, or designer, examined the copy and made other notations to bring the raw material into condition for typesetting. In the desktop medium, the manuscript *is* the typesetting, and the designer's instructions consist of preparatory commands and manipulations on the screen. The text is "poured," from its status as an electronic string, into the conditions set up in the page layout program. The goal is to avoid that second round of keyboarding or retyping.

This means that all editorial changes must be complete before desktop publishing begins. If you're the originator of the text, a few experiences with garbled layouts will pull you quickly into line. But if you're working with writers, editors and other keyboardists, then you must establish a system for preparing the text file for page format.

You'll find yourself as responsible for the condition of the electronic "manuscript" as that old-time printer was, marking up copy with his colored pencils.

With your electronic manuscript in good order, you can turn your attention to setting up your pages. In the next chapter, you'll learn the basic steps for turning your words into text.

CHAPTER TWO

Setting Up Your Text

Setting Up Your Text

In all printed work, words take on various levels of importance, depending on their functions. The text, or "body copy," occupies the most fundamental level. This is the heart of the matter—where the actual reading happens. And your job is to facilitate that reading. Other type elements you use are essentially "display" type: headings, titles, chapter or section openings—usually set in large type sizes. And while they're also meant to be read, their main purpose is to direct the reader smoothly into the text, where the information is.

To organize and structure your text for optimum reading involve a number of steps and decisions—some of which may seem like niggling details that don't really matter. But you'll learn just how important those seemingly minor details can be.

Among these important steps to structuring your text layout are the following:

1. Establish page margin sizes and number of columns.

2. Set line lengths.

3. Select type size and line spacing.

4. Choose an alignment scheme: justified, ragged or mixed.

5. Adjust word and letter spacing as needed.

You may have noticed that typeface selection isn't mentioned in the preceding outline. Although you can certainly start thinking about typeface choices, it's important to establish your page format first.

As we discuss each of these steps in turn, it's important to remember that your decisions regarding the structure of body copy should be made to reflect the kind of work you're producing. In other words, if you're preparing a legal document, your decisions will be quite different from those you'd make for a newsletter devoted to current trends in rock music.

COMPUTERS AND THE LAW

You may have noticed that typeface selection isn't mentioned in the preceding outline. Although you can certainly start thinking about typeface choices, it's important to establish your page format first.

As we discuss each of these steps in turn, it's important to remember that your decisions regarding the structure of body copy should be made to reflect the kind of work you're producing. In other words, if you're preparing a legal document, your decisions will be quite different from those you'd make for a newsletter devoted to current trends in rock music. Your desktop publishing program starts by asking you to specify margins, and it's a logical place to begin. Before you get involved with style and design, you must determine the area the type will occupy within the page—the block of black type in a white space.

Because page makeup programs show you the margins of your pages as a constant, you have the opportunity to play with surrounding white space as an idea before you even begin to lay out your letter or publication. Let's examine the function of margins and how they relate to the text.

Margins are merely a way of defining the positive spaces, even though they're laid out in terms of the negative. The type area is framed with white in order to separate it from the surrounding environment, to facilitate reading by delineating text, to provide consistency and unity when there's more than one page, and to make the thing look nice. You can test the necessity of margins by trimming them off a page. Mass market paperbacks give you an idea of just how little is needed. But you'll notice they cannot be eliminated completely—they're fundamental to legibility.

Setting Margins

Your desktop publishing program starts by asking you to specify margins, and it's a logical place to begin. Before you get involved with style and design, you must determine the area the type will occupy within the page—the block of black type in a white space.

Because page makeup programs show you the margins of your pages as a constant, you have the opportunity to play with surrounding white space as an idea before you even begin to lay out your letter or publication. Let's examine the function of margins and how they relate to the text.

Margins are merely a way of defining the positive spaces, even though they're laid out in terms of the negative. The type area is framed with white in order to separate it from the surrounding environment, to facilitate reading by delineating text, to provide consistency and unity when there's more than one page, and to make the thing look nice. You can test the necessity of margins by trimming them off a page. Mass market paperbacks give you an idea of just how little is needed. But you'll notice they cannot be eliminated completely—they're fundamental to legibility.

You may have noticed that typeface selection isn't mentioned in the preceding outline. Although you can certainly start thinking about typeface choices, it's important to establish your page format first.

As we discuss each of these steps in turn, it's important to remember that your decisions regarding the structure of body copy should be made to reflect the kind of work you're producing. In other words, if you're preparing a legal document, your decisions will be quite different from those you'd make for a newsletter about current trends in rock music. Your desktop publishing program starts by asking you to specify margins, and it's a logical place to begin. Before you get involved with style and design, you must determine the area the type will occupy within the page—the block of black type in a white space.

Because page makeup programs show you the margins of your pages as a constant, you have the opportunity to play with surrounding white space as an idea before you even begin to lay out your letter or publication. Let's examine the function of margins and relations to the text.

Margins are merely a way of defining the positive spaces, even though they're laid out in terms of the negative. The type area must feel as if it is floating correctly. The type area is framed with white in order to separate it from the surrounding environment, to facilitate reading by delineating text, to provide consistency and unity when there's more than one page, and to make the thing look nice. You can test the necessity of margins by trimming them off a page. Mass market paperbacks give you an idea of just how little is needed. But you'll notice they cannot be eliminated completely—they're fundamental to legibility.

You may have noticed that typeface selection isn't mentioned in the preceding outline. Although you can certainly start thinking about typeface choices, it's important to establish your page format first.

As we discuss each of these steps in turn, it's important to remember that your decisions regarding the structure of body copy should be made to reflect the kind of work you're producing. In other words, if you're preparing a legal document, your decisions will be quite different from those you'd make for a newsletter about current trends in rock music.

Your desktop publishing program starts by asking you to specify margins, and it's a logical place to begin. Before you get involved with style and design, you must determine the area the type will occupy within the page—the block of black type in a white space.

Because page makeup programs show you the margins of your pages as a constant, you have the opportunity to play with surrounding white space as an idea before you even begin to lay out your letter or publication. Let's examine the function of margins and relations to the text.

Margins are merely a way of defining the positive spaces, even though they're laid out in terms of the negative. The type area is framed with white in order to separate it from the surrounding environment, to facilitate reading by delineating text, to provide consistency and unity when there's more than one page, and to make the thing look nice. You can test the necessity of margins by trimming them off a page. Mass market paperbacks give you an idea of just how little is needed. But you'll notice they cannot be eliminated completely—they're fundamental to legibility.

Because page makeup programs show you the margins of your pages as a constant, you have the opportunity to play with surrounding white space as an idea before you even begin to lay out your letter or publication. Let's examine the function of margins and relations to the text.

Margins are merely a way of defining the positive spaces, even though they're laid out in terms of the negative. The type area is framed with white in order to separate it from the surrounding environment, to facilitate reading by delineating text, to provide consistency and unity when there's more than one page, and to make the thing look

Margin Size

It's a little harder to tell how wide each of the margins around a text block ought to be. There are several considerations.

One is that the relationship between type and page should be dynamic, active. Notice that if you create equal margins all around, even if they're ample ones, the type area will appear to be in the wrong place on the page: the top margin will look larger than the sides, and the bottom margin too small. The text block will look like it's drooping to the bottom, and there will be a stiffness instead of the lively, energetic page you're trying to achieve.

Because page makeup programs show you the margins of your pages as a constant, you have the opportunity to play with surrounding white space as an idea before you even begin to lay out your letter or publication. Let's examine the function of margins and relations to the text.

Margins are merely a way of defining the positive spaces, even though they're laid out in terms of the negative. The type area is framed with white in order to separate it from the surrounding environment, to facilitate reading by delineating text, to provide consistency and unity when there's more than one page, and to make the thing look nice. You can test the necessity of margins by trimming them off a page. Mass market paperbacks give you an idea of just how little is needed.

So as a beginning rule of thumb, try this: on a single page, make the side margins equal, the top margin slightly less than the sides, and the bottom margin greater (as much as double the size of the top margin). The type area is roughly proportional to the page—a radical departure from this proportion looks bad, too. Since at the early stages the margin shapes are merely malleable grid lines, you can move things around till they are not merely okay, but bang on. Keep trying and you'll begin to see.

Because page makeup programs show you the margins of your pages as a constant, you have the opportunity to play with surrounding white space as an idea before you even begin to lay out your letter or publication. Let's examine the function of margins and relations to the text.

Margins are merely a way of defining the positive spaces, even though they're laid out in terms of the negative. The type area is framed with white in order to separate it from the surrounding environment, to facilitate reading by delineating text, to provide consistency and unity when there's more than one page, and to make the thing look nice. You can test the necessity of margins by trimming them off a page. Mass market paperbacks give you an idea of just how little is needed. But you'll notice they cannot be eliminated completely—they're fundamental to legibility.

One is that the relationship between type and page should be dynamic, active. Notice that if you create equal margins all around, even if they're ample ones, the type area will appear to be in the wrong place on the page: the top margin will look larger than the sides, and the bottom margin too small. The text block will look like it's drooping to the bottom, and there will be a stiffness instead of the lively, energetic page you're trying to achieve.

So as a beginning rule of thumb, try this: on a single page, make the side margins equal, the top margin slightly less than the sides, and the bottom margin greater (as much as double the size of the top margin). The type area is roughly proportional to the page—a radical departure from this proportion looks bad, too. Since at the early stages the margin shapes are merely malleable grid lines, you can move things around till they are not merely okay, but bang on. trying and you'll begin to see that the margins are the frame that set off the text.

An important point to consider is that a single-column page of type demands a different margin treatment than a multicolumn page. This isn't only to avoid excessively long lines on a page (we'll come back to that later) but also because the gutters between columns create bands of white.

Equal margins.

Because page makeup programs show you the margins of your pages as a constant, you have the opportunity to play with surrounding white space as an idea before you even begin to lay out your letter or publication. Let's examine the function of margins and relations to the text.

Margins are merely a way of defining the positive spaces, even though they're laid out in terms of the negative. The type area is framed with white in order to separate it from the surrounding environment, to facilitate reading by delineating text, to provide consistency and unity when there's more than one page, and to make the thing look nice. You can test the necessity of margins by trimming them off a page. Mass market paper backs give you an idea of just how little is needed. But you'll notice they cannot be eliminated completely—they're fundamental to legibility.

One is that the relationship between type and page should be dynamic, active. Notice that if you create equal margins all around, even if they're ample ones, the type area will appear to be in the wrong place on the page: the top margin will look larger than the sides, and the bottom margin too small. The text block will look like it's drooping to the bottom, and there will be a stiffness.

Experimenting with white space.

Margins and Columns

An important point to consider is that a single-column page of type demands a different margin treatment than a multicolumn page. This isn't only to avoid excessively long lines on a page (we'll come back to that later) but also because the gutters between columns create bands of white needed for a dynamic page. You'll notice that a three-column format placed within margins appropriate to a single-column page looks just as peculiar as a single mass of type with a tiny band of white around it.

Because page makeup programs show you the margins of your pages as a constant, you have the opportunity to play with surrounding white space as an idea before you even begin to lay out your letter or publication. Let's examine the function of margins and relations to the text.

Margins are merely a way of defining the positive spaces, even though they're laid out in terms of the negative. The type area is framed with white in order to separate it from the surrounding environment, to facilitate reading by delineating text, to provide consistency and unity when there's more than one page, and to make the thing look nice. You can test the necessity of margins by trimming them off a page. Mass market paperbacks give you an idea of just how little is needed. But you'll notice they cannot be eliminated completely—they're fundamental to legibility.

One is that the relationship between type and page should be dynamic, active. Notice that if you create equal margins all around, even if they're ample ones, the type area will appear to be in the wrong place on the page: the top margin will look larger than the sides, and the bottom margin too small. The text block will look like it's drooping to the bottom, and there will be a stiffness instead of the lively, energetic page you're trying to achieve.

So as a beginning rule of thumb, try this: on a single page, make the side margins equal, the top margin slightly less than the sides, and the bottom margin greater (as much as double the size of the top margin). The type area is roughly proportional to the page—a radical departure

Because page makeup programs show you the margins of your pages as a constant, you have the opportunity to play with surrounding white space as an idea before you even begin to lay out your letter or publication. Let's examine the function of margins and relations to the block of text.

Margins are merely a way of defining the positive spaces, even though they're laid out in terms of the negative. The type area is framed with white in order to separate it from the surrounding environment, to facilitate reading by delineating text, to provide consistency and unity when there's more than one page, and to make the thing look nice.

You can test the necessity of margins by trimming them off a page. Mass market paperbacks give you an idea of just how little is needed. But you'll notice they cannot be eliminated completely—they're fundamental to legibility.

One is that the relationship between type and page should be dynamic, active. Notice that if you create equal margins all around, even if they're ample ones, the type area will appear to be in the wrong place on the page: the top margin will look larger than the sides, and the bottom margin too small. The text block will look like it's drooping to the bottom, and there will be a stiffness instead of the lively, energetic page you're trying to achieve.

So as a beginning rule of thumb, try this: on a single page, make the side margins equal, the top margin slightly less than the sides, and the bottom margin

In determining how many columns to use on a page, the first consideration is content. Your own intuition should tell you whether the nature of a piece demands the appearance of a publication (i.e., a public document); a personal communication, such as a business letter; or a serious book-like text, such as a report.

In some cases, the distinction is none too clear: books in a large format are often set in double columns; the number of columns on a newsletter page can vary widely; and in some kinds of reports, the columns might be hard to distinguish because of the complexity of visual information. We'll return to the structure of columns and their relation to content in several places later on.

The amount of white space needed around a single column of type is in part determined by the nature of the type itself. And as we move forward, you'll discover that none of these decisions, wherever they come in the typographic sequence of your software, can be made in isolation. Type size and style, space between lines and other factors affect the amount of white space needed as a border.

However, there are some ridiculous extremes. In bringing together the elements of type and space, you'll find that while there's considerable flexibility, there are limits beyond which the effect will be somewhat inappropriate. Just as a tiny margin framing long tedious lines of dull gray legalese is excessive, so is a tiny block of oversized letters plunked in the middle of a sea of white. Learning to understand those limits leads you closer and closer to the right choices.

Because page makeup programs show you the margins of your pages as a constant, you have the opportunity to play with surrounding white space as an idea before you even begin to lay out your letter or publication. Let's examine the function of margins and relations to the text.

Margins are merely a way of defining the positive spaces, even though they're laid out in terms of the negative. The type area is framed with white in order to separate it from the surrounding environment, to facilitate reading by delineating text, to provide consistency and unity when there's more than one page, and to make the thing look nice. You can test the necessity of margins by trimming them off a page. Mass market paperbacks give you an idea of just how little is needed. But you'll notice they cannot be eliminated completely—they're fundamental to legibility.

One is that the relationship between type and page should be dynamic, active. Notice that if you create equal margins all around, even if they're ample ones, the type area will appear to be in the wrong place on the page: the top margin will look larger than the sides, and the bottom margin too small. The text block will look like it's drooping to the bottom, and there will be a stiffness instead of the lively, energetic page you're trying to achieve.

So as a beginning rule of thumb, try this: on a single page, make the side margins equal, the top margin slightly less than the sides, and the bottom margin greater (as much as double the size of the top margin). The type area is roughly proportional to the page—a radical departure from this proportion looks bad, too. Since at the early stages the margin shapes are merely malleable grid lines, you can move things around till they are not merely okay, but bang on. Keep trying and you'll begin to see that the margins are the frame that set off the text. One is that the relationship between type and page should be dynamic, active. Notice that if you create equal margins all around, even if they're ample ones, the type area will appear to be in the wrong place

Because page makeup programs show you the margins of your pages as a constant, you have the opportunity to play with surrounding white space as an idea before you even begin to lay out your letter or publication. Let's examine the function of margins and relations to the text.

No breathing room.

Excessive use of white space.

Margins and Facing Pages

Facing pages, such as those in a bound report or brochure, should be treated as a unit, rather than as two separate and distinct parts. In traditional book-making—where some ideas about the disposition of white space go back centuries—the goal is to create a unit in which the margin between the pages is about equal to each of the outer margins, and the bottom margin is about double the top. The type area is in approximate proportion to the page, and if done carefully, there's a kind of logical geometry at work that can be sensed by the person holding the book.

Because page makeup programs show you the margins of your pages as a constant, you have the opportunity to play with surrounding white space as an idea before you even begin to lay out your letter or publication. Let's examine the function of margins and relations to the text.

Margins are merely a way of defining the positive spaces, even though they're laid out in terms of the negative. The type area is framed with white in order to separate it from the surrounding environment, to facilitate reading by delineating text, to provide consistency and unity when there's more than one page, and to make the thing look nice. You can test the necessity of margins by trimming them off a page. Mass market paperbacks give you an idea of just how little is needed. But you'll notice they cannot be eliminated completely—they're fundamental to legibility.

One is that the relationship between type and page should be dynamic, active. Notice that if you create equal margins all around, even if they're ample ones, the type area will appear to be in the wrong place on the page: the top margin will look larger than the sides, and the bottom margin too small. The text block will look like it's drooping to the bottom, and there will be a stiffness instead of the lively, energetic page you're trying to achieve.

So as a beginning rule of thumb, try this: on a single page, make the side margins equal, the top margin slightly less than the sides, and the bottom margin greater (as much as double the size of the top margin). The type area is roughly proportional to the page—a radical departure from this proportion looks bad, too.

Since at the early stages the margin shapes are merely malleable grid lines, you can move things around till they are not merely okay, but bang on. Keep trying and you'll begin to see that the margins are the frame that set off the text. One is that the relationship between type and page should be dynamic, active. Notice that if you create equal margins all around, even if they're ample ones, the type area will appear to be in the test the necessity of margins by trimming them off a page. Mass market paperbacks give you an

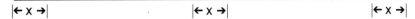

Remember that in any publication with multiple facing pages, the folds and binding must be considered in laying out the margins. A fold is a powerful visual element, and different binding techniques use up varying amounts of space in the "gutter," or binding edge. While you can design a fold on the screen, the technical details of bindery methods and their constraints on your design should be taken up as a production concern early on.

Exploring New Territory

Modern styles have diverged considerably from the classic models, and it's not uncommon to find standard proportions defied in the interest of visual tension or an exciting treatment. This is where squinting and your innate sense of logic and proportion can help. If you're working out an unconventional pattern of white space, step back from it and ask yourself dispassionately if the thing coheres, if the manipulation of white space actually aids in the presentation of the information. If you're in doubt, you can always retreat to the conventional. No one will be put off by simple, traditional margins.

A final word about setting margins is that they should be consistent to facilitate reading. Your page layout program encourages this consistency by treating margins as a global setting. In fact, it's important to maintain consistency in the arrangement of white space at all levels of typographic assembly.

Readers will accept daring layouts only if they accommodate the process of reading and comprehension. If you're exploring new territory in the disposition of black and white, following an idea through rather than scattering your effects will keep the reader involved and enhance the document's design continuity.

White Space

Considering the problem of white space generally, I think you could say that more is better. Even a tiny block of type on a big page looks, and reads, better than words densely packed with a tiny border. Even a single large letter on a page creates a field of white interrupted by unusual and random shapes that give pleasure to the eye.

Once you begin to see white space as a dynamic function in your pages, as being equally important with the black letters and words, you'll be able to judge how much white space is good and how to create a consistent pattern for the pages of your publication. Then you'll have the thing at your mercy.

Line Length and Type Size

Despite some interesting experiments in other modes over the centuries, reading—and therefore typesetting—is linear. It's a convention going back to the beginnings of the alphabet. And by the time the Roman alphabet was established, the convention of the rigid left-hand margin was also firmly implanted in our reading habits. These two traditions have become the rule in typesetting, at least in the setting of text, and you mess around with them at your typographic peril.

But sticking to traditional text alignment doesn't mean sacrificing an interesting layout. You have many other devices to choose from to add variety and dynamics to your work. There are, however, some rules of thumb:

Line Length

Lines can be just about as long as you want them, if they have enough leading (or line spacing) between them so the reader can find the next line when returning to the left margin. However, there's a limit to the number of words the reader can comfortably follow, so the type should not be too small for the length of the line. Lines of type can be too short as well, with the type size too large. Either case hinders pleasurable reading. So type size, line length and interlinear space are intimately connected.

If you are having a lot of trouble getting justified columns to look good, the culprit may well be that lines are too short or type too large. There is an optimum average number of words to a line for smooth justification, and that number varies according to the typeface and the page program you're using. Try setting the type one point size smaller, retaining ample leading for ease of reading. Or switch to a typeface with a narrower set.

Lines can be just about as long as you want them, if they have enough leading (or line spacing) between them so the reader can find the next line when returning to the left margin. However, there's a limit to the number of words the reader can comfortably

If you are having a lot of trouble getting justified columns to look good, the culprit may well be that lines are too short or type too large. There is an optimum average number of words to a line for smooth justification, and that number varies according to the typeface and the page program you're using. Try setting the type one point size smaller, retaining ample leading for ease of reading.

Reducing type size can provide a solution to justification problems.

In columns set ragged-right, you tend to assume everything will fall into place nicely—that word spacing will stay uniform and manually inserted hyphens used sparingly will keep the ragged line endings proportionate. But it's not always that simple.

You may find that the columns seem narrower than you expected. This effect happens because automatic column guides constrain the text to a maximum width within the measure you've specified. I often find that increasing column widths just a bit beyond the guides improves the look of the whole column.

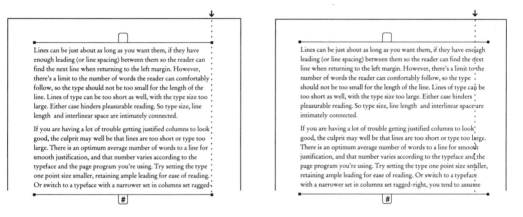

Type Size

If you're accustomed to working on a typewriter or word processor, you have two sizes of type in your mind's eye. "Pica"- size typewriter faces correspond to 12-point type (they set 10 characters to the inch), and "elite" sizes are roughly the size of 10-point type (or 12 characters to the inch). These terms have endured from the old English type-size vocabulary.

You are accustomed to adjusting line length according to these sizes, and you have an idea how many words should fit. This is because each letter in a typewriter alphabet occupies the same amount of space as every other, whereas in typesetting, characters occupy space according to their natural configuration—an i is much narrower than an m, for example. Therefore, you find that the number of words that fit on any given line increases dramatically.

```
The difference between
typewriter output and type-
set material has played
havoc with the conventions
of certain kinds of docu-
ments, especially business
correspondence and reports
```
Typewriter

The difference between typewriter
output and typeset material has
played havoc with the conventions
of certain kinds of documents,
especially business correspondence
and reports on standard business
paper—the lines of type on those

Typesetting

The difference between typewriter output and typeset material has played havoc with the conventions of certain kinds of documents, especially business correspondence and reports on standard business paper—the lines of type on those pages have just too many words in them!

Letter Shapes and Proportions

Two other structural characteristics affect the type size, line length and leading. It's in the nature of type design that within a given point size the letters may be drawn larger or smaller, as well as wider or narrower. These significant variables in the drawing affect how much line spacing and margins they need in order to look good.

These variables are discussed in technical and aesthetic terms later in the book, but for now, notice this: If type is "small on the body," it will accommodate more words to a given line and point size, and have more apparent space between lines, than a face that is "large on the body." A face that "sets narrow" will crowd in more words to a line than a face that "sets wide." These variables affect legibility in small type sizes and the fitting of copy to a given space.

"The best mirror is an old friend." German Proverb

"The best mirror is an old friend." German Proverb

Bembo sets more words to a line than the same type size of Stone.

Your problem as a desktop publisher is to bring all these variables together into a pleasing whole.

Generally, the larger the type size the better, and the more space between lines the better. Of course, large type and increased leading may mean your copy won't fit the space allowed for it in your design. And there are ridiculous extremes at which point the text loses its appropriateness or visual coherence.

Line Spacing

Typists are accustomed to limited line spacing options: usually, the half-line increment is the only alternative to the pre-set space between lines. Typesetting systems, on the other hand, allow a wide range of settings, even in tiny increments, making possible very subtle interlinear space adjustments.

M anipulating spacing can be a little trickier than it first appears. Page programs handle leading in different ways, and maintaining alignment and getting the appearance right depend on where the additional space is placed. Usually it's added either below the type line or proportionately above and below. If you have a choice, consistently adding leading below

9-point type

9-point leading

M anipulating spacing can be a little trickier than it first appears. Page programs handle leading in different ways, and maintaining alignment and getting the appearance right depend on where additional space is placed. Usually it's added either below the type line of proportional above and below. If you have a choice, consis-

9-point type

10-point leading

M anipulating spacing can be a little trickier than it first appears. Page programs handle leading in different ways, and maintaining alignment and getting the appearance right depend on where additional space is placed. Usually it's added either below the type

9-point type

12-point leading

Manipulating line spacing can be a little trickier than it first appears. Page programs handle leading in different ways, and maintaining alignment and getting the appearance right depend on where the additional space is placed. Usually it's added either below the type line or proportionately above and below. If you have a choice, consistently adding leading below the type line will make life simpler.

<u>Manipulating line spacing can</u>
<u>be a little trickier than it first</u>
<u>appears. Page programs handle</u>
<u>leading in different ways, and</u>

Baseline leading.

Manipulating line spacing can
be a little trickier than it first
appears. Page programs handle
leading in different

Proportional leading.

In some programs leading increments may be proportionate to type size—another snare to the unwary perfectionist. Proportional leading might work well if the text is all one type style and size. But as soon as any other element is added, it becomes tedious to reconcile visual and mechanical spacing.

Stick to point-specific leading and always add it to the bottom (check your style commands for these adjustments) and always measure from the head of the type, or from baseline to baseline.

In the world of fine printing—much of which is still done with lead type—pages are expected to back each other up perfectly, line for line throughout. You'll occasionally see an aficionado hold up a book page to check the "backup." Such precise alignment is probably more than we can expect from laser printers, copying machines and offset duplicators. But if our work at least strives for that precision on the screen, it will be pleasing to an ordinary reader, as a perfect backup is to a book lover.

Alignment

Whatever the text you're setting, whatever the typeface you choose, a decision must be made about whether to set the columns in perfectly rectangular blocks, in which the lines are justified, or to let the line endings be uneven, creating a ragged margin.

Justification

Justified margins come from a tradition older than printing. Ancient handwritten books have cleverly adjusted, perfectly even margins—

all done by eye. Printed books and then newspapers followed the convention. Contemporary style accepts ragged margins in all areas of publication. In most cases, however, justified margins accommodate more type to a column; and nowadays, with space at a premium, most books and newspapers are set this way.

Justification involves allocating space among words and relying heavily on word hyphenation at line endings to make each line exactly the same length as all others. Digital page layout programs can automatically perform these functions, and much of the memory required by desktop publishing is devoted to their sophisticated hyphenation dictionaries.

Most programs allow you to manipulate hyphenation zones to some degree to increase or decrease space between words. Professional dedicated typesetting equipment has even more extensive hyphenation capabilities, as well as precise control over space between words and letters, to avoid awkward white gaps.

Another problem results when consecutive hyphenated line endings create a string of hyphens along the right-hand margin. Convention demands no more than three consecutive right-margin hyphens: and if you get a bad row of them, you'll see the problem. This too must be repaired.

Awkward word spacing.

Another problem results when consecutive hyphenated line endings create a string of hyphens along the right-hand margin. Convention demands no more than three consecutive right-margin hyphens: and if you get a bad row of them, you'll see the problem. This too must be repaired.

Tight word spacing.

And those white gaps can be a problem. It occasionally happens that because a line is short and a word won't break, word spacing increases abnormally. When this occurs in several consecutive lines, a vertical "river" of white space may develop, creating a distraction and causing the reader's eye to wander. You can find these rivers by squinting or by turning the page upside down and then squinting. They have to be repaired.

Another problem results when consecutive hyphenated line endings create a string of hyphens along the right-hand margin. Convention demands no more than three consecutive right-margin hyphens; and if you get a bad row of them, you'll see the problem. This too must be repaired. Convention demands no more than three

Rivers.

Another problem results when consecutive hyphenated line endings create a string of hyphens along the right-hand margin. Convention demands no more than three consecutive right-margin hyphens; and if you get a bad row of them, you'll see the problem. This too must be repaired. Convention demands no more than three consecutive

Rivers repaired.

Another problem results when consecutive hyphenated line endings create a string of hyphens along the right-hand margin. Convention demands no more than three consecutive right-margin hyphens; and if you get a bad row of them, you'll see the problem. This too must be repaired.

Another problem results when consecutive hyphenated line endings create a string of hyphens along the right-hand margin. Convention demands no more than three consecutive right-margin hyphens; and if you get a bad row of them, you'll see the problem. This too must be repaired. Convention demands no more than three consecutive right-margin

Excessive hyphenation.

Another problem results when consecutive hyphenated line endings create a string of hyphens along the right-hand margin. Convention demands no more than three consecutive right-margin hyphens; and if you get a bad row of them, you'll see the problem. This too must be repaired. Convention demands no more than three

Minimal hyphenation.

The problems encountered in justifying type—bad spacing and excessive hyphenation—can usually be solved by adjusting word spacing and kerning values or, occasionally, adding a word break not found in the program dictionary. As a further refinement, a word space can be replaced after a period with a thinner space (usually requiring a command keystroke). The combination .T is a good example. Other letter combinations lend themselves to spacing adjustments if automatic character compensation fails to solve the problem; for example, l l appears to have less word space than the combination y v.

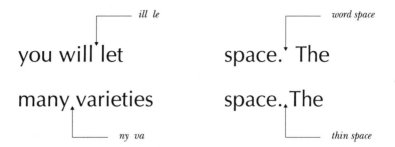

If the problem can't be solved by such adjustments, a last resort would be to edit or transpose text.

You must be willing to persevere for the sake of appearance if you hope to make really good-looking pages. You'd be surprised how important these tiny adjustments are in the subliminal responses of your readers. You should develop an understanding with the source of your text, the writer and/or editor, that such alterations may be necessary.

Flush-Left/Ragged-Right

The other common way to set text is "flush-left, ragged-right," as it's commonly known in type terminology. This is considered by many typographers—among them the great lettering artist Eric Gill, writing in his *Essay on Typography*—to be a more pleasing and coherent way to set text. The space between words remains constant so the flow of reading is not interrupted. Inequities in spacing fall at the ends of lines, where they lend a kind of natural texture and variety to the pages.

This doesn't mean that adjustments are never needed to lines of ragged text. A well-balanced column is important, so you must avoid excessive variation in line length. The right-hand margin should follow an arbitrary, average limit that gives form to the text block.

While some believe that hyphenation should be avoided completely, in most cases it's necessary to hyphenate occasionally for appearance—and I've even done minor rewriting now and then to make a ragged column of type look better. Most of us have had some experience with setting up correspondence of various kinds on typewriters or word processors; and the function of balancing ragged margins in publications isn't much different from making a letter look good on the page.

The other common way to set text is "flush-left, ragged-right," as it's commonly known in type terminology. This is considered by many typographers—among them the great lettering artist Eric Gill, writing in his *Essay on Typography*—to be a more pleasing and coherent

The other common way to set text is "flush-left, ragged-right," as it's commonly known in type terminology. This is considered by many typographers—among them the great lettering artist Eric Gill, writing in his Essay on Typography—to be a more pleasing and coherent way to set text. The space between words remains constant so

Unbalanced right margin.

Balanced right margin.

Formality and Informality

There's a kind of informality to pages set ragged-right that must be considered in your overall design scheme. While you can give almost any kind of asymmetrical or daring treatment to a heading over justified columns, it's virtually impossible to combine formal, centered display lines over columns set ragged-right, without creating an incongruous effect. The asymmetry of ragged settings demands that the display material follow that dynamic imbalance of black and white.

**KEY AWARDED
AT FORMAL DINNER**

There's a kind of informality to pages set ragged-right that must be considered in your overall design scheme. While you can give almost any kind of asymmetrical or daring treatment to a heading over justified columns, it's virtually impossible to combine formal, centered display lines over columns set ragged-right, without creating an incongruous effect. The asymmetry of ragged

**KEY AWARDED
AT FORMAL DINNER**

There's a kind of informality to pages set ragged-right that must be considered in your overall design scheme. While you can give almost any kind of asymmetrical or daring treatment to a heading over justified columns, it's virtually impossible to combine formal, centered display lines over columns set ragged-right, without creating an incongruous effect.

A consistently formal design treatment works better than one that attempts to combine formal, centered display lines with an informal ragged-right column.

For centuries, the conventions of typography demanded justified margins, centered display headings and formal layouts, although all along there were places where the dynamics of asymmetry could be found, such as in the glorious decorated initial letters and other rubrication of early printed books. In our era, the visual tension of asymmetrical typography has been embraced and thoroughly pursued and codified by the designer Jan Tschichold. The studied disposition of black and white masses on a page, unusual formats and typefaces, and constant experimentation give our work a breadth of potential unknown in the days of classical proportions.

But there's something deeply satisfying and comfortable about a page set up according to the formal considerations of the great printed books. And if you're uncertain about your ability to see the dynamics at work in an asymmetrical page, then no one will blame you for sticking to tradition.

TRADITION

But there's something deeply satisfying and comfortable about a page set up according to the formal considerations of the great printed books. And if you're uncertain about your ability to see the dynamics at work in an asymmetrical page, then no one will blame you for sticking to tradition.

But there's something deeply satisfying and comfortable surrounding a page set up according to the formal considerations of the great printed books. And if you're uncertain about your ability to see the dynamics at work in an asymmetrical page, then no one will blame you for sticking to tradition. But there's something deeply satisfying and comfortable about a page set up according to the formal considerations of the great printed books. And if you're uncertain about your ability to see the dynamics at work in a page, then no one will blame you for sticking to tradition.

A WAY OF LIFE

But there's something deeply satisfying and comfortable surrounding a page set up according to the formal considerations of the great printed books. And if you're uncertain about your ability to see the dynamics at work in an asymmetrical page, then no one will blame you for sticking to tradition. But there's something deeply satisfying and comfortable about a page set up according to

Formal, symmetrical page format.

TRADITION

But there's something satisfying and comfortable about a page set up according to the formal considerations of the great printed books. And if you're uncertain about your ability to see the dynamics at work in an asymmetrical page, then no one will blame you for sticking to tradition.

But there's something deeply satisfying and comfortable about a page set up according to the formal considerations of the great printed books. And if you're uncertain about your ability to see the dynamics at work in an asymmetrical page, then no one will blame you for sticking to tradition. But there is something deeply satisfying and comfortable about a page set up according to the formal considerations of the great printed books. And if you're uncertain about your ability to see the dynamics at work in a page, then no one will blame you for sticking to tradition.

A WAY OF LIFE

But there's something deeply satisfying and comfortable about a page set up according to the formal considerations of the great printed books. And if you're uncertain about your ability to see the dynamics at work in an asymmetrical page, then no one will blame you for sticking to tradition. But there's something deeply satisfying and comfortable about a page set up according

Flush-left, ragged-right page format.

The middle ground is setting everything flush-left/ragged-right— both headings and text blocks. This scheme is common in newsletters and other business publications. By using this straightforward approach you can stick to an accepted method while learning how the natural shapes of words and lines create energetic and unusual white shapes around them. Then, as your confidence grows, you'll be ready to begin making use of other treatments to achieve visual tension and variety.

Flush-Right/Ragged-Left

I noticed recently a page that consisted almost entirely of a huge illustration with type run all around it (easy to do with sophisticated layout programs). The type on the right side of the page was set all ragged-left, and in this case flush-right, but it could have been ragged on both sides. While this creates a dramatic effect (if you squint), I'd like to point out that, except in short hits, setting ragged-left—whatever the right margin—slows the reader down to a crawl. The convention of the firm left-hand margin is a strong one.

Word Spacing

One of the most persistent myths about desktop publishing (along with the one about last-minute changes) is that you can merely pour the copy in and forget about it.

The reality is that the work will have that finished quality you desire only if you're willing to make some minor adjustments to the poured text. Whether the setting is justified or ragged, the desired appearance is what calligrapher Edward Johnston called a "general uniformity of flow" to the text. There are a few minor techniques and tricks for achieving this.

Usually, if you've set reasonable parameters for justification in your program, the worst offenders in spacing will be lines with bad breaks, caused by long single-syllable words (e.g., through and though) or word breaks not included in your program's hyphenation dictionary. The narrower the column, the more likely problems

Usually, if you've set reasonable parameters for justification in your program, the very worst offenders in hyphenation will be lines with bad breaks, caused by long single-	Usually, if you've set reasonable parameters for justification in your program, the very worst offenders in hyphenation will be lines with bad breaks, caused by long single-syllable words

Narrow columns often look better with manual hyphenation, rather than your program's automatic hyphenation feature.

are to occur. The simplest solution is to manually hyphenate a word; this recomposes the whole type block, usually for the better.

Another problem you may encounter stems from the fact that *mechanically* uniform word spacing isn't necessarily *visually* uniform. Some letter combinations create an illusion of increased or decreased space, making the affected word spaces appear too wide (and occasionally too narrow) compared to the rest of the line.

A typical example is a period followed by a cap W (e.g., n. W), or vertical letters (e.g., lowercase l and lowercase i) at the end and beginning of successive words in display type. In some combinations, eliminating the word space entirely is a solution.

My taxes were late. Wishing I were somewhere else, all I could do was to fill in the blanks!

My taxes were late. Wishing I were somewhere else, all I could do was to fill in the blanks!

In a large mass of text, and for certain kinds of work, the result may not warrant the time spent at this fussy business. As a rule, the larger the type size, the more precision your work requires, and the more bothersome these inequities of spacing will appear. A squint at a first proof will usually show the worst offenders; you can fix them with manual spacing commands and kerning.

Note: While "too much" is the most common and obvious problem in word spacing, it's also possible to have too little. The best-looking setting is usually tight; consequently, setting word-space parameters on the narrow side occasionally produces a line in which the words run together. By holding a page proof upside down, you can test whether a line has enough space between words. You can also detect the "rivers" more easily.

Letter Spacing—Tracking and Kerning

When type characters were made of lead, the way each letter fit in with all the others was constrained by its base—its walls of metal. The designer attempted to position each letter in its domain of rigid space so that it would fit gracefully and legibly with any other member of the alphabet that came before or after it in the composition of words. Some of the old type designs have better fitting characters than others.

Since the days of programmed typesetting, a common solution to unsightly word spacing caused by bad line breaks has been to letter-space the entire line to fit the measure—you see it in newspapers all the time.

> Since the days of programmed type-setting, a common solution to unsightly word spacing caused by bad line breaks has been to letter-space the entire line to fit the measure—you see it in newspapers all the time.

> Since the days of programmed typesetting, a common solution to unsightly word spacing caused by bad line breaks has been to letter-space the entire line to fit the measure—you see it in newspapers all the time.

Most typographers, however, consider letter-spacing lowercase type unacceptable. The great type designer Frederic W. Goudy said, "A man who would letter-space lowercase would steal sheep."

Alas, most page programs have this last-resort capability built into their justification style modes; so it's up to you to hold to the greater truth and ignore it. It's preferable to rewrite, but the screen is so flexible it's usually possible to hyphenate your way around a really bad break, or adjust space between certain letter combinations.

Tracking

In the digital medium, each character occupies not a fixed but an arbitrary space. Therefore, the fitting of letters can be deliberately adjusted. Overall character fitting is called *tracking*. Fitting between specific pairs of individual characters is called *kerning*.

A typeface as you find it on disk has been constructed with tracking appropriate to the typeface design, with each letter presumably spaced to fit properly with every letter in the typeface alphabet. But typemakers are not infallible. Some typeface versions may not be well fitted, and it would be appropriate to make tracking adjustments.

Most publishing programs let you adjust tracking to accommodate spacing or appearance requirements. It's not uncommon to see tracking, especially in advertising copy, tightened up until all the letters bump together. On the other hand, in order to justify columns, sometimes tracking is allowed to run loose.

KeepaCoolHead

Tight tracking.

Keep a Cool Head

Loose tracking.

There's a natural fit among the letters of a particular type design, a natural balance that should be maintained. And if the tracking is altered too severely, the space between letters looks wrong in relation to the space inside the letters. Bad tracking can make a good type design look awful.

There's a natural fit among the letters of a particular type design, a natural balance that should be maintained. And if the tracking is altered too severely, the space between letters looks wrong in relation to the space inside the letters. Bad tracking can

Good tracking.

There's a natural fit among the letters of a particular type design, a natural balance that should be maintained. And if the tracking is altered too severely, the space between letters

Bad tracking.

The worst offense is to tighten up the overall space around letters to the point that they lose their distinct relationships in all their various combinations. On the other hand, the built-in spacing is optimized for a small range of sizes. Unconventional sizes of almost any design will benefit from tightening (if they're larger than usual) or loosening (if set particularly small). If you mess with tracking, proof your work carefully.

Kerning

It's in the nature of the alphabet that some letters do not fit together well. Even in the old days, certain characters were kerned, or cast to hang over the edge of their metal sides, in order to make them fit their companions.

Certain combinations of capitals (WA, for example), some uppercase and lowercase combinations (such as Wa or To), and some letters combined with punctuation (y.) are the most common candidates for kerning. Typefaces and page makeup programs allow access to a number of automatic kerning pairs, fewer or more depending on the source. And it's possible in most programs to create additional pairs for special circumstances.

WA	Want	Tonight	any.
WA	Want	Tonight	any.

Letter-spacing commands in your program allow you to increase or decrease space between letters on an individual basis, and this is necessary in any line set in all capitals. Large display lines of any kind may demand minute changes in the relationship of individual characters in the interest of appearance.

Spacing Around Those Pesky Points and Figures

"Points" (punctuation marks) and "figures" or "figs" (numbers) can be aggravating elements in typography, however essential they are. Often, their shapes create awkward white space around them. Before the days of automatic kerning pairs, punctuation invariably upset the flow of text lines, and even today it's often necessary to adjust space to make points look better.

Be sure it's clear that punctuation belongs to whatever is being punctuated (initials, such as P. W., for example). Close up space where the white "hole" above periods and commas is a problem. Open up the space before exclamation points ("scare points"), especially after verticals such as l and i; use thin spaces between ellipsis points for uniform appearance (. . . rather than ...).

Wherever possible, make these typographic adjustments a part of your program style sheets or part of the word processing digital "manuscript." (Many digital fonts have an ellipsis character that can be accessed from the keyboard.)

you will! Today.

you will! Today.

you will...

you will…

Quotation marks can also cause problems. In most fonts, opening quotes and closing quotes are two distinct characters and differ in appearance. Be sure to put each in the proper place.

You may also find it necessary to "hang" a quote mark in the margin of some kinds of text when it's the first character of the line. This is easier to do now, with kerning commands, than it used to be. Hanging punctuation wherever it interrupts the clean line of a margin is a mark of careful and attentive typography, but it takes some trial and error to handle it properly.

"Life seems to me like a
Japanese picture which our
imagination does not allow to
end in the margin."
                Oliver Wendell Holmes

"Life seems to me like a
Japanese picture which our
imagination does not allow to
end in the margin."
                Oliver Wendell Holmes

Opening quotation mark aligned.

Hanging opening quotation mark.

Figures, too, can be worrisome. In most desktop typefaces, the figures (or figs) are the same height as the capitals, creating a disconcerting effect. A few fonts now have "old style" figures, which more closely follow the flow of the ascenders and descenders of lowercase letters. Wherever possible, these old style figs should be used in text. The "lining" figures work well with all caps and in tabular work. Fractions are also beginning to appear as font characters, so you don't have to use those terrible built-up fractions of the early systems. I'd suggest switching faces to find these improvements if the job you're doing is loaded with numbers.

As margins, columns, alignment, typeface, sizes and spacing specifications are established, your project begins to have form and framework. Each component complements and strengthens every other. It may take some trial and error to make this happen, but the rewards will be satisfying.

CHAPTER THREE

Choosing a Typeface

Choosing a Typeface

Okay. You've been dancing around, itching to get into typefaces for two chapters now—and here they are. As you advance through the intricacies of desktop publishing, you'll spend a lot of time getting to know the names and distinguishing characteristics of typefaces and how to choose them to reflect the tone and spirit of your piece.

Out of the many hundreds of faces available, you'll find that some are used often, others rarely. Some faces are appropriate for almost any purpose, while others are so peculiar they fit only specific jobs. You'll also discover there are some you like and some you can't stand—and those won't necessarily be the same as mine.

Bitstream's Old Dreadful No. 7, a typeface you might use only for special occasions.

There are also a few typefaces that seem hard to avoid using, since they're standard with all desktop publishing systems—based, I think, on a perceived universal popularity. Proprietary versions of Helvetica and Times Roman form most beginners' impressions of typefaces.

And while they're useful for many simple jobs, and demonstrate the wide design variations that exist, these faces must be seen as rudimentary at best, an invitation to boring pages at worst.

What Is a Typeface?

A typeface is a family of letters all of the same design. The differences in design between two typefaces are often minute; but all the members of a single typeface will cohere and go well together on the page, because they're based on a single design scheme. A typeface comprises various fonts, which include uppercase and lowercase alphabets, figures and punctuation.

A typeface family can include as many as a dozen or more fonts; a simple family unit contains four fonts—roman, italic, bold and bold italic. You can always tell what a font is because that's what your printer considers an individual component. Century Schoolbook is a typeface. Century Schoolbook Bold Italic is a font.

New Century Schoolbook

New Century Schoolbook Italic

New Century Schoolbook Bold

New Century Schoolbook Bold Italic

With few exceptions, the contents of a contemporary type font duplicate the upper and lower cases of those ancient printing houses. For your purposes in setting the text of a publication, you can remember that a font comprises all the characters you can enter from the keyboard without a command, plus small caps. (Actually, small caps exist only in the roman font, and most programs treat them as reduced sizes of the capitals. They are used sparingly.)

Different typeface designs come about through a combination of the artisan's creativity and the cultural demands of the time. It's usually the designer who gives a typeface its name and, of course, its individual character. But in fact, it is through relating a typeface's development to a historical period that it can be categorized and understood.

In order to establish a frame of reference for understanding typeface history and design, we need to look at some basic distinctions among typefaces.

Serif Type

A fundamental division of type styles is between serif (roman) and sans-serif faces. These are a couple of the most esoteric-sounding terms you'll run across in this study, but no matter where you've begun to explore desktop publishing, chances are you've already learned something about this distinction in basic type styles, usually through some form of Times Roman (sometimes called "Dutch") and Helvetica (sometimes called "Swiss"), a sans-serif face.

"The French will only be united under the threat of danger. Nobody can simply bring together a country that has 265 kinds of cheese."

Charles de Gaulle

Times Roman, Dutch

"The French will only be united under the threat of danger. Nobody can simply bring together a country that has 265 kinds of cheese."

Charles de Gaulle

Helvetica, Swiss

A serif is a "finishing stroke," an embellishment similar to those used in all the utilitarian arts—architecture and interior design, pottery, masonry and the like. But in typography, finishing strokes are practical as well. They play a very important part in the appearance and style of the typeface and the readability of

265 kinds of cheese

the text. As we progress through a gathering of types, you'll see how this is so. There's a tremendous variety in serif shapes.

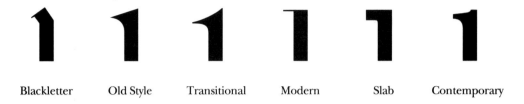

| Blackletter | Old Style | Transitional | Modern | Slab | Contemporary |

Traditionally, upright type with serifs is called roman, and the slanted variation that usually accompanies a roman face is called italic. The italic is actually an individual letterform, although the differences are obvious only in the narrow, arched quality of the drawing and in a few of the characters, such as the lowercase a and g. Some types have such unusual serif shapes that they're given other classifications, such as "slab serif" or "Egyptian." We'll return to some of these variants later on.

Garamond is a serif typeface.
Garamond Italic is a serif typeface.

Sans-Serif Type

Sans-serif types, or types without serifs, are not merely roman types with the serifs removed. They actually represent a different approach to letterforms, only part of which is in the lack of finishing strokes. Italic versions are usually just sloped forms of the upright letters and have no appreciable design differences.

Helvetica is a sans-serif typeface.
Helvetica Italic is a sans-serif typeface.

Another point of terminology and lore: You've probably been wondering about the origin of the terms "uppercase" and "lowercase" letters. Years ago, when all type was set by hand, the leaden letters were arranged in cases, on a sloped work bank. The frequently used small, or "minuscule," alphabet was placed near at hand, while the case containing the letters used less often—the "capitals," small capitals, figures and punctuation—were placed above. Hence, the "upper and lower cases." How traditions persevere in language!

And finally, a note on type classification. Many attempts have been made to organize the vast array of typefaces from all the ages into groupings, or categories, of shapes and styles. Because of the huge libraries of types amassed by the digital "foundries," the variants often get classified right back into chaos. Not everyone agrees on the boundaries of the classes, either, and without strong historical or geographical identifying characteristics, the classifications become blurred. In the interest of simplification, I've kept to the broadest outlines. So what follows shouldn't be seen as classification but as an introduction. As you work, classifications become less significant.

A Thumbnail History of Type

Type forms have a rich and complex past that we should respect as the source of the beauty of the roman letter we know today. If you're interested in letterforms, you'll probably want to explore their history further. (The great two-volume set, *Printing Types: Their History, Forms and Use*, by Daniel Berkeley Updike [available from Dover Paperbacks, bless their hearts], remains the standard introduction.)

The first types were modeled after a particular regional handwriting style, which didn't persist very long after printing spread out into the world. Although the types of the Gutenberg Bibles have yet to be surpassed in sheer beauty of form and the effect of their mass in text columns, the lettering style itself as a model has been relegated to decorative use. Perhaps someday this writing and typeface style we call "blackletter" will return to favor, and pages will regain some of the visual power of those early printed books.

The story of type for our purposes starts with the handwriting style of the Italian Renaissance and moves quickly to mid-16th century France. It was during these 50 years or so that the fundamentals of the typographic form were established, as printing spread rapidly throughout Europe, and books were made at an astonishing rate.

Out of these early days of printing, the general category of typefaces we know as the Old Style evolved.

Old Style

The Old Style is important for the number of its representatives alone. There are more revivals from Old Style than from any other period; and contemporary designs based on Old Style models abound. From its origins in Venice in the late 15th century, the Old Style developed through most of western Europe and England until the mid-18th century, when styles began to change noticeably toward a more modern face. Old Style designs didn't follow a progressive path. Nor did they die out at a particular time or place. History is never a straight line.

Old Style faces are characterized by serifs and shapes reminiscent of the pen-drawn forms on which they were based. Those pens were held at about a 30 to 45 degree angle to the writing line, creating oblique strokes and angular, wedge-like serifs. There's a kind of moderation between thick and thin strokes resulting from the pen's drawing angle. The effect gives a generally mellow appearance to a page of text.

Typography.

Italian Old Style

As the Old Style developed through time and place, the contrast between thick and thin gradually increased, while the oblique slant to the strokes decreased. What we see when we look at a series of types through history is that thick strokes become slightly thicker, thins become thinner, and there's an overall increase in the "color" these various types create in a text block. Much of this change was the result of ongoing improvements in metallurgy, ink, paper-making and other printing technologies, and later on in press construction.

The illustration shows a progression of Old Style faces, from 16th century Italy through France, Holland and England—some notable contemporary reconstructions and reinterpretations from the 250 years of printing and type design.

Bembo   Typography.

Garamond   Typography.

Janson   Typography.

Caslon   Typography.

For text setting, the Old Style faces offer a range of possibilities for tone and color on the page. Bembo and Garamond project a rather subdued, "classical" look. Janson is more dynamic and Caslon, pleasantly quirky. Of the four, Caslon has the most noticeable "personality," which might make it inappropriate for certain kinds of work, and Garamond probably has the broadest range of utility for standard desktop printers. Janson keeps growing in favor in my eyes for its robust color and the excellent digital version available. But the face doesn't really look its best at lower resolution printing and wants some advances in the medium for maximum clarity.

Transitional Designs

Late in the 18th century, typeface design began to shift away from the Old Style concept toward what we now call Modern. The most notable examples of this Transitional classification are the designs of the English printer John Baskerville. Characteristics of Baskerville's faces are increased brilliance, a more horizontal tendency of the thin, curved serifs, and almost total absence of the angularity of the broad-pen tradition.

Typography.

New Baskerville

Baskerville looks good in larger sizes and with the ample leading needed for business correspondence and single-column reports on standard paper. Baskerville is also widely used in book and magazine work. Although it's still a very popular face, some find it a little bland, a little too complacent for contemporary applications.

Modern

In Europe, especially France, type took a little different path from the Dutch and English, ever tending toward a delicate, refined look. By the beginning of the 19th century, this transition from the Old

Style to Modern was complete in all regions. It was the Italian printer Giambatista Bodoni who created the archetype of modern faces, with thin, perfectly horizontal serifs, powerful thick strokes and fragile thin strokes throughout.

The result of this extreme contrast on the page was increased brilliance along with a more rigid shape. It's ironic that some of the brilliance of those early printed books, with their heavy blacks and graceful thins, should return in such a different spirit. Try putting some Bodoni Bold next to a rendition of blackletter for an interesting perspective on the history of letterforms.

Typography.

Bodoni

Use Bodoni with care—the extremes of its thicks and thins won't abide sloppy setting. And bad spacing can make a page of Bodoni look terribly disjointed. For good color, however, there's no other face to match it.

Century, a kind of Transitional Modern face, expresses, at least to me, ultimate simplicity in reading. Not to imply that your readers are dumb, but you can use it for straightforward, unpretentious text.

Typography.

Century

Of course, type design didn't stop evolving at the dawn of the era of steam, and what we classify as "modern" types are anything but modern compared to the work done in this century—especially in this post-industrial era of digital design. The Old Style reappears in contemporary representations; the Modern is reinterpreted as an idea over time.

Typography.

Melior

Slab Serifs

The quality of printing during the 19th century deteriorated with the advent of power machinery, paper manufactured from wood fiber, and the growth of journalism and print advertising. Careful craftsmanship took a back seat to mass production.

Our most notable heritage out of those days, aside from the persistence of a few modern typefaces, is the grand array of decorative type styles that were produced. This was the era of the "Egyptian" slab serif faces, some of them so bold and condensed there was hardly a white space. It was the time of the "western" decorative faces reminiscent of ghost towns and cattle rustlers. We still draw on the library of floriated, human-figured, illustrated letters that were invented in the name of decoration.

Typography.

Memphis

Typography.

Clarendon

Typewriter faces are largely modeled after Egyptian's type forms; they all set a monotone line you must be wary of in dense text settings. The Clarendon shapes are more varied and interesting than the pure slab serifs; but overall I think the role of these faces in text work is limited.

Old Style Revivals

By the end of the 1800s, those involved in good printing had begun to rediscover the great typefaces of the past. The invention of machine type-casting and setting was followed by several decades of modern re-creations of the best work of the world's great presses and designers. Those revivals led to the new reinterpretations of today, and provided a coherent history of modern lettering and type design that have given us the incredible wealth of typographic imagery we have captured in our small computers.

Times Roman	Typography.
Goudy Old Style	Typography.
Galliard	Typography.
Sabon	Typography.

As we dig further into type designs, the name Goudy will recur, for despite the rise and fall of typographic fads, his work endures. His Old Style is anything but a slavish copy of a historic face. While it has its limits, it's so downright good looking that it's used extensively. The bold font is one of the best.

Look at Times for an interpretation of the spirit of the same Dutch Old Style represented by Janson—with good contrast of thick and thin, good color on the page. But some feel that Times, originally intended only for high-quality newspaper text, has been interpreted to death.

Sabon is designer Jan Tschichold's most effective rendition of Garamond.

Emergence of Sans-Serif Type

Although sans-serif faces first appeared during the age of steam, we can consider this design approach as contemporary, beginning as successful experiments by lettering artists Edward Johnston and Eric Gill in the Teens and Twenties, evolving toward the immensely popular designs of Frutiger, Meidinger and Zapf in the Fifties. As with the design concepts of the roman alphabet, so it is with the reinvention of the approach called "sans," and designers in the digital medium continue to find new ways of looking at the problem.

Optima   Typography.

Gill Sans   Typography.

Helvetica   Typography.

Univers   Typography.

You can see at a glance that these four sans faces represent entirely different approaches to the form, and they give entirely different qualities to a page of text.

I consider Optima one of the greatest typefaces ever, and would choose it over the other three for text setting.

The Gill is a little dated for much contemporary work, although it's perfectly readable in mass.

I would relegate the Helvetica to only certain kinds of display work or the kind of fine print you want readers to ignore.

Contemporary

While we associate the sans-serif library with the 20th century, there are a number of roman face designs that also express our own time, rather than merely evoking or replicating earlier forms. The best exponent of this modern design I've been calling "contemporary" is probably Palatino. One of the most widely known, used and copied typefaces of any era, Palatino has been successfully translated and standardized into the digital medium and is available on most desktop systems. The drawing of its serifs, stems and bowls makes Palatino an excellent model for comparing the same identifying characteristics in historical typefaces and in "contemporary" faces as they appear.

Palatino   Typography.

Stone Serif   Typography.

The only fault I can find with Palatino is that it "sticks its elbows out," as my teacher, the lettering artist John C. Tarr, put it, meaning it sets rather wide in the line. Otherwise, the shapes, modeling and overall elegance of Palatino make it one of the enduring faces of this century. And to make up for its width, notice how readable it is in small sizes.

Stone, designed for digital media at all resolutions, is definitely a hip typeface. It has the advantage of a huge interconnected family that includes a sans and an "informal," and a variety of weights to cover all kinds of needs. It is somewhat limited by being excessively large on the body.

Most of the faces you've just seen are discussed in greater depth in Chapter 6, "Building Your Type Library." This quick look gives you an idea of how you can direct the tone of a page with nothing more than the text face you choose; how you as the typographer can use these major stylistic models and choose among the qualities expressed by different type designs to accurately convey your message.

Allusive Typography

The famous book designer Bruce Rogers coined the term "allusive typography" to denote the use of period types, decoration and other effects when setting up books from the past. His work is a remarkable study for the expression of this concept and creative typography in general. But I would like to borrow the term and place it in a wider context. Although few of us are involved in producing period pieces, using specific type styles to "allude" to the content and spirit of a text can be helpful.

You see how typeface design proceeded from Renaissance elegance, to the robust Dutch and English Old Style, through the Transitional forms of John Baskerville and into the contrast of color and form in Bodoni's modern faces. And you've seen the 20th century bring reinterpretations of all these, as well as the introduction of sans types and new approaches to serif and stem.

I hope this historical perspective on the evolution of type will give you some clearer pictures and new adjectives to describe type forms. The more you're able to find descriptive terms, however inexact, for the text you're setting up, the easier it will be to choose a typeface that expresses some of those characteristics. Is the text fragile or robust? Should the tone be hard-hitting and businesslike to sell roller bearings? Or, do you need a more aesthetic orientation to complement a piece of fiction?

Remember, you're not making judgments, you're making typography—which isn't to put down selling roller bearings. But there's certainly a difference between reading the data in a parts catalog and reading a short story. And those differences should be expressed in the text face as well as in the titles and headings that go with it.

Some Faces Do Everything

If you aren't comfortable with this approach, if it seems a little too mysterious or esoteric, remember that a number of typefaces in the collection have a broad appeal that make them appropriate for almost any kind of text you can come up with.

The reason Times Roman appears on virtually every desktop printer is because of its universal application. Times was designed as a newspaper face (The *Times* of London). Its large size on the body and clear shapes make it eminently legible, in spite of adverse design and production conditions, although it looks its best only under ideal conditions.

It is also generally true that within reasonable limits, any text can be set in any typeface. You shouldn't feel pressured to pursue all the possible choices to come up with the perfect match of type to content. It bears repeating that a good balance of image and space—margins, leading and type size—is far more important to good design than the choice of the typeface.

One reason Times is ubiquitous is because it has little personality, and I guarantee it won't take long for you to find it monotonous and dull. For many, real typography begins when Times gets boring.

It's also very important to like the typefaces you're working with. And I hope it's clear with all this "allusive" business that what I mean is not that you need to pick out a new typeface every time you come up against a new typographic situation.

There's a handful of solid, dependable text faces that will serve adequately for many typographic projects. Some of them, such as Times, Palatino and Century, are already in your printer's system. If you add others as you come to appreciate them, your library will grow useful rather than merely cumbersome.

As you begin to see your texts in terms of typefaces (and I think you will if you stick with it), you'll find yourself attracted to typefaces just as you are to people. It's this sensitivity to appropriateness and a real affection for the letterforms on the part of the designer that produce typography folks actually read.

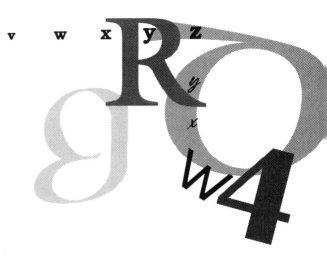

CHAPTER FOUR

Adding Display Type

Display Face Options

While it's fashionable, especially in magazine design, to seek out the most outlandish contrast between text type and headings, you'd be wise to pause before you run off to order from the type catalogs, and consider your basic typeface families and their role in organizing levels of presentation. It helps to know the way families work.

Uppercase Text Font

The uppercase letters of the standard roman font can be set in lines of all capitals to indicate subsidiary breaks in a text, but they're not very strong visually and tend to give a rather sedate air to the piece. To look really good, they must be letter-spaced (see "Letter-Spaced Capitals" on page 73), which tends to weaken their impact if they're set in the text size. Capital letters with small caps can be used and treated pretty much as all-cap lines. Page layout programs allow a variety of sizes in cap and small-cap combinations.

most outlandish contrast between text type and headings, you'd be wise to pause before you run off to order from the type catalogs, and consider your basic typeface families and their role in organizing levels of presentation. It helps to know the way families work.

UPPERCASE TEXT FONT
The uppercase letters of the standard roman font can be set in lines of all capitals to indicate subsidiary breaks in a text, but they're not very strong visually and tend to give a rather sedate air to the piece. To look really good, they must be letter-spaced (see "Letter-Spaced Capitals" on page 73), which

Italic Text Font

The italic forms of the text face also lack the visual punch necessary for a heading. Italics normally work best in their traditional role within the text to provide contrast for quoted sections and special treatment of words or phrases. They usually don't work well in mass;

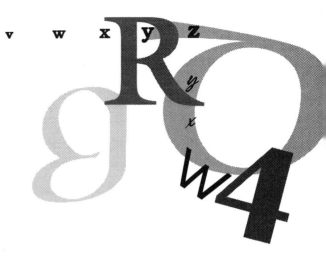

Adding Display Type

Adding Display Type

Now that you've laid out preliminary margins, chosen a typeface, and examined line length, leading and other space relationships—what's next?

A page of solid, uninterrupted text, no matter how well set, isn't particularly appealing. It gives no relief to the eye, no contrast and no cues to designate levels of importance. The only place we'll put up with such uninviting pages is in certain books, such as novels. So, the next thing to do is break up the text into portions, to make it easier and more interesting to read.

You might say that everything that isn't text is display, including photo captions, page numbers, running heads, subheads and pull-quotes. In a sales catalog, for example, all the words might be considered display, if the entries are seen more as reference than as continuous text.

To create contrast, ease of access and visual variety, display type can be used to delineate the parts and draw the reader into the material. Display type is often a larger size or a bold version of the text face, or a contrasting style. Display sizes and faces organize the information for the reader, so there's a strong editorial function involved.

Display Face Options

While it's fashionable, especially in magazine design, to seek out the most outlandish contrast between text type and headings, you'd be wise to pause before you run off to order from the type catalogs, and consider your basic typeface families and their role in organizing levels of presentation. It helps to know the way families work.

Uppercase Text Font

The uppercase letters of the standard roman font can be set in lines of all capitals to indicate subsidiary breaks in a text, but they're not very strong visually and tend to give a rather sedate air to the piece. To look really good, they must be letter-spaced (see "Letter-Spaced Capitals" on page 73), which tends to weaken their impact if they're set in the text size. Capital letters with small caps can be used and treated pretty much as all-cap lines. Page layout programs allow a variety of sizes in cap and small-cap combinations.

most outlandish contrast between text type and headings, you'd be wise to pause before you run off to order from the type catalogs, and consider your basic typeface families and their role in organizing levels of presentation. It helps to know the way families work.

UPPERCASE TEXT FONT

The uppercase letters of the standard roman font can be set in lines of all capitals to indicate subsidiary breaks in a text, but they're not very strong visually and tend to give a rather sedate air to the piece. To look really good, they must be letter-spaced (see "Letter-Spaced Capitals" on page 73), which

Italic Text Font

The italic forms of the text face also lack the visual punch necessary for a heading. Italics normally work best in their traditional role within the text to provide contrast for quoted sections and special treatment of words or phrases. They usually don't work well in mass;

you must experiment. Of course, there are places where whole settings in italics are commonly used, such as announcements and menus.

most outlandish contrast between text type and headings, you'd be wise to pause before you run off to order from the type catalogs, and consider your basic typeface families and their role in organizing levels of presentation. It helps to know the way families work.

Italic Text Font

The uppercase letters of the standard roman font can be set in lines of all capitals to indicate subsidiary breaks in a text, but they're not very strong visually and tend to give a rather sedate air to the piece. To look really good, they must be letter-spaced (see "Letter-Spaced Capitals" on page 73),

Text Font Size

Most page layout programs allow type size variations in minute increments. This can be a way to make use of a text face, its caps and italics in some very subtle display settings. Remember that setting larger lowercase letters, or mixing larger uppercase and lowercase letters, can produce more visual impact than lines of all caps. And lines of large-size uppercase and lowercase italics, such as Stone, Garamond and Janson, can be very effective for headings within a body of text.

most outlandish contrast between text type and headings, you'd be wise to pause before you run off to order from the type catalogs, and consider your basic typeface families and their role in organizing levels of presentation. It helps to know the way families work.

Uppercase & Lowercase Text Font

The uppercase letters of the standard roman font can be set in lines of all capitals to indicate subsidiary breaks in a text, but they're not very strong visually and tend to give a rather sedate air to the piece. To look really good, they must be letter-spaced (see "Letter-Spaced Capitals"

Boldface Text Font

Often the best choice in long blocks of copy, subheads set in bold—
even in the same size as the text face—not only give the eye some
breaks from the relentless gray mass, but can also help organize and
orient the reader. These boldface subheads can act as an outline to
the material. This is particularly true in those tedious seas of gray
print you often find in newsletters and reports. I advocate inventing
subheads if necessary, merely to break up the mass.

As with italics, masses of boldface lose their effectiveness because the
advantage of contrast is lost.

If you keep in mind that the roman lowercase is designed to be the
most readable, you'll leave yourself with the maximum number of
variables for display type: contrast in size, contrast in shape (the
italic) and contrast in color with the bold.

most outlandish contrast between text type and headings, you'd be
wise to pause before you run off to order from the type catalogs, and
consider your basic typeface families and their role in organizing
levels of presentation. It helps to know the way families work.

Boldface Text Font
The uppercase letters of the standard roman font can be set in lines
of all capitals to indicate subsidiary breaks in a text, but they're not
very strong visually and tend to give a rather sedate air to the piece.
To look really good, they must be letter-spaced (see "Letter-Spaced

For the large sizes needed for titles and headlines, there's always
safety in the basic text face at any level of visual importance. And
you'll be surprised and gratified at how much color and variation
you can wring out of the basic alphabets of the simplest type family.

Spacing Display Type

Just as important as the contrast of style and color is the handling of
white space to set off headings, break up text blocks and create
interesting shapes on the page. A subhead set in bold may have the

color you want; but if it's run in as just another line of text, it doesn't help much in creating visual relief. Sometimes merely providing half a line of space above and below the subhead is enough to set it off and make it dynamic.

Headings within the text should be spaced for continuity of reading as well as for consistent line spacing and margins. There should be slightly less space below a head than above it, so it will connect with the text that follows. And the space allowed for a heading should equal some multiple of the line spacing used in the text. For example, if both your text and heading are set 11 on 12 (11-point type on 12 points of lead), you might want to put an 8-point line of space above the head and a 4-point line below, to match the text spacing and keep the head attached to the text that follows. Notice that all-cap lines may need to be spaced differently than uppercase and lowercase lines with their descenders. Heads set in larger sizes should still occupy space equal to line-spacing increments.

most outlandish contrast between text type and headings, you'd be wise to pause before you run off to order from the type catalogs, and consider your basic typeface families and their role in organizing levels of presentation. It helps to know the way families work.

Well-Spaced Display Type

The uppercase letters of the standard roman font can be set in lines of all capitals to indicate subsidiary breaks in a text, but they're not very strong visually and tend to give a rather sedate air to the piece. To look really good, they must be letter-spaced (see "Letter-Spaced Capitals" on page 73),

Avoid crowding, and remember that more white space is generally better than less. If you're not happy with the heads as you have them set up, try increasing space around them. If space is at a premium (as it often is in publishing), try gaining white space by reducing the type size by one point, either in the text or in the headings. The effect of extra white space may make up for the loss in size. Don't forget to save each version, just in case.

Alignment of Heads

Titles and headings may be positioned almost anywhere on the column, sometimes across more than one column or even across more than one page. But there are some conventions that apply, depending on the situation and on the typographic style.

Flush-Left

The most natural position of heads, at all levels, is flush-left and ragged-right. This is true whether the text columns are set ragged or justified, and applies to heads set in uppercase and lowercase, all caps, or (occasionally) all lowercase. Flush-left heads appear most at home above ragged columns; this is the informal style. They also seem to like the informality of uppercase/lowercase settings.

Notice two things about headings set to the left margin. One is that phrases can be broken more naturally than in other styles, which seems to create a more graceful flow to the words of the headings. The other is that white space is grouped in a random shape to the right of the head, where it has a dynamic visual impact.

two things about headings set to the left margin. One is that phrases can be broken more naturally than in other styles.

Heading Set Flush-Left

The other is that white space is grouped in a random shape to the right of the head, where it has a dynamic visual impact. Notice two things about headings set to the left margin. One is that phrases can be broken more naturally than in other styles, which seems to create a more graceful flow to the words of the head-ings. The other is that white space is grouped in a random shape

The lines of flush-left headings should be broken in logical ways, so they read well and balance visually. They look funny if they're top-heavy, if connecting words are left dangling or if words have to be hyphenated. Rewriting is often necessary for good balance.

Ragged-Left and Mixed

The informal style has further possibilities. Heads can be placed flush to the right-hand margin or mixed according to the visual dynamic of the letters and the space. Here white space is at your disposal, and the interaction of black and white will be either dynamic or static according to your choices of type size, weight and placement.

For example, look at what happens to negative space around a heading if you shift to a flush-right alignment, leaving the left margin ragged. The reader's eye must follow an unpredictable course. If this effect is handled properly, it can really make your pages come alive under the right circumstances. I warned earlier that you won't want to carry this unusual treatment too far; the eye relies heavily on returning to a common left-hand margin to make reading flow along quickly, so it's an inconvenience in anything but heads and short bursts of text, such as captions for illustrations.

two things about headings set to the left margin. One is that the phrases can be broken more naturally than in the other styles.

This Heading Set Flush-Right on a Flush-Left Column

The other is that white space is grouped in a random shape to the right of the head, where it has a dynamic visual impact. Notice two things about headings set to the left margin. One is that phrases can be broken more naturally than in other styles, which seems to create a more graceful flow to the words of the headings. The other is that white space is grouped in a random shape

In some situations, such as advertising, certain title pages, announcements and flyers—all essentially display settings—it's acceptable to manipulate type purely on the basis of visual balance and tension. Without the constraints of a consistent margin treatment, and where long passages of continuous reading aren't demanded, you can experiment with the arrangement of display type.

You might try making both margins ragged, or vary indentions from a common margin for different type block elements. Avoid scattering the pieces, and remember as you develop your ideas that the elements in the layout must have some relation to one another, some logic that can be seen in the finished whole.

Headings, Margins & Columns

The other is that white space is grouped in a random shape to the right of the head, where it has a dynamic visual impact. Notice two things about headings set to the left margin. One is that phrases can be broken more naturally than in other styles, which seems to create a more graceful flow to the words of the headings. The other is that white space is grouped in a random

Type treated in this way becomes somehow pictorial. The page escapes from the geometric rigidity of consistent columns and margins, and approaches the loose, impulsive quality of drawing or splashing ink about. At the same time, language, and therefore type, is logical and sequential; and if you don't keep both the logic and the looseness in mind simultaneously, one will be lost and the reader will be confused.

I once heard a famous architect, talking about house interiors, say, "Group your effects!" What that means in typographic terms is that if you give reason to the position of a line on the page—usually by echoing that same position somewhere else—there will be logic to the construction by that very relationship. Remember "squinting" from Chapter 1? In designing these purely visual layouts, step back and ask yourself if the type coheres on the page. Can you give a reason for putting each element where it is? Will somebody else be able to see the reason, however subtle? Don't cling to a design so tricky no one else can figure it out.

Centered Headings

When columns are justified, centered heads can be appropriate, if the text will accommodate this formal, rather subdued treatment. Centered lines create a symmetry of black and white. The "tombstoning" of centered lines set in all caps was the universal style for title pages and chapter openings in books for centuries, and you can still see remnants of this visual imagery where the "classical" mode is being followed. You also see this design approach in such unlikely places as *The New York Times.*

HEADINGS SET CENTERED ON THE COLUMN

The other is that white space is grouped in a random shape to the right of the head, where it has a dynamic visual impact. Notice two things about headings set to the left margin. One is that phrases can be broken more naturally than in other styles. The other is that white space is grouped in a random shape to the right of the head, where it has a dynamic visual impact. Notice two things about headings set to the left margin. One is that phrases can be broken more naturally than in other styles, which seems to create a more graceful flow to the words of the headings. The other is that white space is

Several points should be kept in mind if you want to use centered heads. First, notice that they just won't work on top of text columns set ragged-right. Rarely can the symmetrical and the asymmetrical be brought together effectively; in this case, the balanced white spaces of the head are contradicted by the grouped and random white shapes of the column. Try it.

Several points should be kept in mind if you want to use centered heads. First, notice that they just won't work on top of text columns set ragged-right. Rarely can the symmetrical and the asymmetrical be brought in.

THIS HEADING SET
CENTERED ON A
FLUSH-LEFT COLUMN

Notice two things about headings set to the left margin. One is that phrases can be broken more naturally than in other styles. The other is that white space is grouped in a random shape to the right of the head, where it has a dynamic visual impact. Notice two things about headings set to the left margin. One is that phrases can be broken more naturally than in other styles. The other is that white space is grouped in a random

Next, notice the importance of the spaces around and between centered lines. If the lines are too nearly the same length, or staggered too radically, then the grace of the symmetry is lost. If there's too little space between the lines, the letter spacing, word spacing and line spacing all conflict and the heads look merely inept. Also, you'll see that while it's not exactly wrong to center headings set in uppercase and lowercase, the more natural form is all caps.

**THIS HEADING IS
CENTERED WITH THREE
VARIED LINES**

And, finally, lines set in all caps should be *letter-spaced* for a balanced appearance. This is especially true of roman caps. The idea is to create the appearance of equal space between every letter in the line, and the process goes like this: Some character combinations, such as IH or NN, should have thin spaces added between them, and others, such as AV or WA, should be kerned more closely together. There are certain letter combinations, such as RA or WY, which cannot be effectively adjusted, in which case all other letter spacing must be increased to match that awkward set. And, finally, lines set in all caps should be *letter-spaced* for a balanced appearance. This is especially true of roman caps. The idea is to create the appearance of equal space between every letter in the line, and the process goes like this: Some character

**THIS IS A HEADING
THAT IS CENTERED
WITH EQUAL LINES**

And, finally, lines set in all caps should be *letter-spaced* for a balanced appearance. This is especially true of roman caps. The idea is to create the appearance of equal space between every letter in the line, and the process goes like this: Some character combinations, such as IH or NN, should have thin spaces added between them, and others, such as AV or WA, should be kerned more closely together. There are certain letter combinations, such as RA or WY, which cannot be effectively adjusted, in which case all other letter spacing must be increased to match that awkward set. And, finally, lines set in all caps should be *letter-spaced* for a balanced appearance. This is especially true of roman caps. The idea is to create the appearance of equal space between every letter in the line, and the process goes like this: Some character

**This Heading Has Uppercase
and Lowercase Type**

And, finally, lines set in all caps should be *letter-spaced* for a balanced appearance. This is especially true of roman caps. The idea is to create the appearance of equal space between every letter in the line, and the process goes like this: Some character combinations, such as IH or NN, should have thin spaces added between them, and others, such as AV or WA, should be kerned more closely together. There are certain letter combinations, such as RA or WY, which cannot be effectively adjusted, in which case all other letter spacing must be increased to match that awkward set. And, finally, lines set in all caps should be *letter-spaced* for a balanced appearance. This is especially true of roman caps. The idea is to create the appearance of equal space between every letter in the line, and the process goes like this: Some character

Letter-Spaced Capitals

And, finally, lines set in all caps should be *letter-spaced* for a balanced appearance. This is especially true of roman caps. The idea is to create the appearance of equal space between every letter in the line, and the process goes like this: Some character combinations, such as IH or NN, should have thin spaces added between them, and others, such as AV or WA, should be kerned more closely together. There are certain letter combinations, such as RA or WY, which cannot be effectively adjusted, in which case all other letter spacing must be increased to match that awkward set.

ILLUSTRATE

ILLUSTRATE

Letter-spacing capital letters can create a more balanced look.

Letter-spacing cannot be done by formula and requires experimentation to find the right balance. Space between words must be increased as well when letter-spacing, or the words will appear to run together. A proof and corrections are usually required to make letter spacing come out right. Done properly, lines of letter-spaced caps can be very beautiful.

It's sometimes the case that the opposite is done, especially in lines of sans-serif caps. Here, the space is tightened so that some combinations actually overlap or run together. This style is more often used when the lines are set flush-left; it takes advantage of the dynamic of letter shapes, perhaps at the expense of legibility. Another style letter-spaces each line of caps to the full width of the margin, and in title pages and major headings uses varying sizes of caps from line to line to make them fill the measure. These different treatments can have a profound effect on the tone of a page.

Kerning

There is an important relationship between the mechanical and the visual in display settings. On one hand, the display lines have to fit the constraints of column size, leading and alignment. On the other hand, the word or group of words you've chosen may not fit exactly into the limits you've set up.

In such cases, do not be afraid to adjust for appearance, especially in headings.

Below are some examples:

Some capital letters (e.g., T,W,V) will need to be kerned toward the left-hand margin or else they'll look somewhat inset. Kerning combinations that look good at text sizes are often not tight enough for display sizes, without manually kerning certain letter combinations. It's not unusual to manually kern an entire line of display type.

In centered heads, punctuation and some of the angled letters may cause the line to look unbalanced, even though it's mechanically correct. If it doesn't look perfectly centered, you have to fix it. As mentioned earlier, increasing word spacing between letter-spaced caps keeps them from appearing to run together.

"Tschichold's Typography"
An Asymmetric Analysis

"Tschichold's Typography"
An Asymmetric Analysis

Effective display type creates visual impact—it attracts the eye. Words and meanings can be instantly recognized. It's a different kind of legibility than that demanded by the long business of reading text. You need to be more sensitive to the white space as well as the black type, particularly in headings, since more than anything else the reader is attracted by a lively and appropriate balance between the two. Time spent refining this visual image is repaid with headlines that really work.

Mixing Typefaces

When they're all variations of the same text face, large sizes, boldface, caps and italics have a kind of predictability. They lend a natural coherence to the document. But by the same token, they don't enrich the piece you're doing with any contrast of idea, whatever the variations in shape and tone you're able to achieve. Even with a large extended family like Stone (18 members), Univers with 20 or more versions or Cheltenham (you'll have to look this one up), the designers' ideas are all essentially repeated throughout every series: they're intended to be coherent, after all.

Stone Serif ▪ *Stone Serif Italic* ▪ Stone Serif Semibold ▪ *Stone Serif Semibold Italic* ▪ **Stone Serif Bold** ▪ ***Stone Serif Bold Italic*** ▪ Stone Sans ▪ Stone Sans Italic ▪ Stone Sans Semibold ▪ *Stone Sans Semibold Italic* ▪ **Stone Sans Bold** ▪ *Stone Sans Bold Italic* ▪ Stone Informal ▪ *Stone Informal Italic* ▪ Stone Informal Semibold ▪ *Stone Informal Semibold Italic* ▪ **Stone Informal Bold** ▪ ***Stone Informal Bold Italic***

The Stone typeface family

To expand your typographic ideas, the obvious step is to pick a companion face that augments those ideas, surprises the reader by extreme contrast of shape and weight, or carries the burden of establishing a feeling of tone or style when the text face doesn't. Or you may add a companion typeface for purely decorative purposes.

Mixing Typefaces

When they're all variations of the same text face, large sizes, boldface, caps and italics have a kind of predictability. They lend a natural coherence to the document. But by the same token, they don't enrich the piece you're doing with any contrast of idea, whatever the variations in shape

Mixing Typefaces

When they're all variations of the same text face, large sizes, boldface, caps and italics have a kind of predictability. They lend a natural coherence to the document. But by the same token, they don't enrich the piece you're doing with any

Some Rules of Thumb for Combining Typefaces

While contrast isn't the only criterion for combining two different typefaces, it's the easiest to address, and the safest. Two faces that are truly different won't produce the embarrassing muddle often seen in careless design. As we've observed with the bold version of a text face in display sizes, extreme contrast in weight is another good way to judge a secondary typeface.

One of the most well-known sets of companion faces (at least to desktop publishers) is Times Roman for a text face and Helvetica for heads. There was a time when that was about all you could get on these systems, and it's still a surprisingly popular combination. Curiously, it works rather well. The two faces are diametrically opposed in structure, and far enough apart in style and historic implication that the distinctions between the two are very clear. And they're a model for contrasting type combinations: roman for text face and sans-serif for headings.

Combining Typefaces

When they're all variations of the same text face, large sizes, boldface, caps and italics have a kind of predictability. They lend a natural coherence to the document. But by the same token, they don't enrich the piece you're doing with any contrast of idea, whatever the

The popular Helvetica headline/Times Roman text face combination.

Avoid a hodgepodge of color, tone and letter shape that's likely to cause visual confusion. An extreme example would be to mix Baskerville with Janson, Caslon or Bodoni Book. These faces, being from adjacent stylistic periods, create a visual dissonance that will be noticed by even the most unsophisticated reader.

On the other side of this, you might mix Baskerville with Bodoni Poster—maybe even with Bodoni Bold if there were enough difference in the sizes—and get away with it, since the greater contrast and the shapes of these extreme versions of Bodoni aren't as closely related to Baskerville. I don't think even the bold weights of *any* Old Style face would be distinct enough from Baskerville to work in headings. Ugly.

Old Style Typefaces

When they're all variations of the same text face, large sizes, boldface, caps and italics have a kind of predictability. They lend a natural coherence to the document. But by the same token, they don't enrich the piece you're doing with any

Old Style Typefaces

When they're all variations of the same text face, large sizes, boldface, caps and italics have a kind of predictability. They lend a natural coherence to the document. But by the same token, they don't enrich the picce you're doing with any

So one of the most important rules of thumb is to avoid confusion of period or history. You don't want to appear unaware of the difference both visually and historically between two faces by creating an effect like the sound of two adjacent piano keys played simultaneously.

Also, avoid a crowd of faces all vying for attention. Depending on your project, you can sometimes get away with more than one secondary display face. Newsletters, for example, seem able to accommodate a variety of type styles if the material to be presented isn't too complex. For books and serious reports, however, where you want to set a single stylistic tone overall, a third face can begin to clutter. I'll never forget my teacher, Adrian Wilson, tsk-tsking over a title page I'd set with one line in an errant face.

Rules of Thumb

So one of the most important rules of thumb is to avoid confusion of period or history. You don't want to appear unaware of the difference both visually and historically between two faces by creating an effect like the sound of two adjacent piano keys played simultaneously.

Avoiding a Crowd of Faces

Also, avoid a crowd of faces all vying for attention. Depending on your project, you can sometimes get away with more than one secondary display face. Newsletters, for example, seem able to accommodate a variety of type styles if the material to be presented isn't too complex. For books and serious reports,

Three different typefaces in one document is often one too many.

Be sure your intent is clear. A decorative face might fit nicely with the layout you're assembling but totally miss the point of the text. A face normally associated with circus posters won't go over very well in a report to the board of directors. Likewise, flowery letters for the steel industry, extra-bold mechanical-looking stuff for a daycare center flyer—that sort of thing. This is really just an extension of the idea of allusiveness in typography; but here it's more vital, since display type carries so much of the burden for setting the tone of the piece. All three of these examples could be set in the same text face, but probably no single secondary face for heads would be appropriate for all of them.

Typesetters Bored With "Directors" Meeting

Be sure your intent is clear. A decorative face might fit nicely with the layout you're assembling but totally miss the point of the text. A face normally associated with circus posters won't go over very well in a report to the board of directors. Likewise, flowery letters for the steel industry, extra-bold mechanical-looking stuff for a daycare center flyer—that sort of thing.

UniSteel MegaCorp Forges Ahead

Be sure your intent is clear. A decorative face might fit nicely with the layout you're assembling but totally miss the point of the text. A face normally associated with circus posters won't go over very well in a report to the board of directors. Likewise, flowery letters for the steel industry, extra-bold mechanical-looking stuff for a daycare center flyer—that sort of thing.

Tots-A-Lot Skips Recess

Be sure your intent is clear. A decorative face might fit nicely with the layout you're assembling but totally miss the point of the text. A face normally associated with circus posters won't go over very well in a report to the board of directors. Likewise, flowery letters for the steel industry, extra-bold mechanical-looking stuff for a daycare center flyer—that sort of thing.

Finally (and I've said this before) rely on your own sense of good taste. Bad combinations tend to look bad. In the old days, there was some excuse for bad typography because type libraries were limited;

and once a series of heads was set up by hand, only the most dedicated would go back through and change them all just because they didn't look quite right. Nowadays, there's no excuse.

But what about unconventional relationships between faces? We've looked at some of the popular combinations; for example, Helvetica and Times. It's much less common to see the reverse of the two: Helvetica or some other sans for text, and Times or other roman face for display type. It can be argued that since every piece of visual language is different, the unusual typographic combos are merely those we haven't seen or thought of yet. But as you're winging along, applying these rules of thumb (with some grains of salt), keep in mind that text is to read, and the visual gaffes are your own.

Sizing Display Type

In setting up the text of a piece, legibility within the space available dictates type size and all the other constraints we've discussed. But what about the size of display faces? Is there a way to know what size goes where and in what circumstances? It's pretty obvious when heads of a certain kind are too small, but how do you know if they're too big?

One of the most useful features on my page makeup system lets me plink the type size of heads up and down by one-point increments. Who ever heard of 39-point type in the old days? Plink! 38-point, et cetera. Later, we'll look at your computer screen as a kind of mobile layout pad, where you put these digital capabilities to the test. But for now, let's look at this size variability and its relation to the uniformity of your design.

How Big, How Small?

First, obviously, what fits. Columns are constraining—they do more than any design scheme to limit the size of heads. If you can afford only a single line, your variables are type size and rewriting. I said that it's obvious when a headline is *too small*; this is really a matter of the use of space. There's a difference between merely putting a line or two in a given space, and making those lines look as though they belong in the space they occupy. Make the space work for you rather than letting it become an inert scrap of paper with something printed on it.

Big Heading

A first concern is relationships. If you have a complex system of heads and subheads, the size of each level must be carefully chosen and maintained to help the reader understand quickly where he or she is in the hierarchy of information.

Medium Heading

Logic, too, dictates that you don't have a giant head stuck in someplace for no apparent reason. Heads must be appropriate to the subject matter. Big heads, however interesting, would be inappropriate to a legal document.

Tiny Heading

They would also be inappropriate in a situation where they looked gratuitous; for example, if they made the copy look padded out to fill more space than required.

It's harder to tell what's *too big*. Letters create interesting spaces, and I find myself tempted to set larger, to capture interesting shapes inside and around the letters. I'd rather go bigger than bolder.

Relationships

A first concern is relationships. If you have a complex system of heads and subheads, the size of each level must be carefully chosen and maintained to help the reader understand quickly where he or she is in the hierarchy of information. Logic, too, dictates that you don't have a giant head stuck in someplace for no apparent reason. Heads must be appropriate to the subject matter. Big heads, however interesting, would be inappropriate to a legal document. They would also be inappropriate in a situation where they looked gratuitous; for example, if they made the copy look padded out to fill more space than required.

PART ONE

They would also be inappropriate in a situation where they looked gratuitous; for example, if they made the copy look padded out to fill more space than required. Heads must be appropriate to the subject matter.

PART TWO

Big heads, however interesting, would be inappropriate to a legal document. They would also be inappropriate in a situation where they looked gratuitous; for example, if they made the copy look padded out to fill more space than required.

Consistency

Finally, the size of heads must be consistent at each level of editorial importance. Otherwise, the reader cannot easily tell the logic of the sequences. Even minor variations in size will be noticed, if only subliminally. So it's best to avoid the temptation, given the capability, to bump a display line up or down a size or two to make it justify or balance, if it thereby loses conformity with heads of the same order of importance.

Pull-Quotes and Sidebars

Pull-quotes are short quotations pulled from the text of an article and set in a larger type size. Their purpose is to catch the eye and help break up a page or column of type. Sidebars are short articles related to and designed to be placed adjacent to larger feature articles.

These devices are especially popular in newsletter and magazine design—in the world of multicolumn grids. I mention them here because they're good examples of typographic tricks that can look great and work poorly. I'm referring to meaningless pull-quotes that merely interrupt the flow and sidebars that don't seem to relate to anything.

I like pull-quotes that read in sequence across the face of a dense piece—as a substitute for subheads—that stimulate the reader's interest and provide a quick synopsis of the text. When they don't say anything, they don't work. If they look bad, they don't work.

The wrong type size and style, too much or too little white space, overuse of gray screens, borders and boldface can be deadly. Rather than popping enthusiastically out of the text mass, they look like separate islands of mediocrity in a sea of gray. Large italics of the text face work well, with no more than a line space above and below. And if there are no interesting quotes to pull, don't bother.

> *"I like pull-quotes that read in sequence across*
> *the face of a dense piece—*
> *as a substitute for subheads—that stimulate*
> *the reader's interest..."*

A sidebar won't work if it looks like a separate and distinct article; it must relate to a larger item to be effective. Visually, an effective treatment is to use a grid in which the feature covers, say, two or three of five columns, and the sidebar, one or a half column. Tints, screens and boxes can be used to frame the sidebar, but they must not increase its visual importance to something more appealing than the feature itself. And they must actually relate to the feature article—or again, why bother?

All these so-called "rules" have exceptions, of course, and only the specific project at hand will provide the framework for a correct approach. In a page of display type only (for example, a title page or a printed advertisement), many decisions will be dictated by the overall "picture" you're trying to create. In such cases, subtle variations may well be appropriate and fit the logic and tone of the thing precisely.

CHAPTER FIVE

Type as Ornamentation and Graphics

Type as Ornamentation and Graphics

*Y*ou can go quite a distance toward making your pages appealing and readable with nothing more than text, headlines and the appropriate manipulation of white space. But the desire to do more, to dress up those pages, can often be overwhelming.

To satisfy this urge, the designer adds diagrams, drawings and photographs, while the typographer looks to the rich repertory of pictorial shapes found in typeface designs to add finishing touches.

Decorative Initial Letters

You've already seen how display sizes for type can help organize a page, but it's also possible to use large letters as pure decoration. Used in unexpected ways, even the most restrained text typeface has decorative possibilities.

Ornamental initial letters go back to the earliest days of the European illuminated manuscript, where they were works of art in themselves—intricately drawn, elaborately colored, often burnished in gold. In the early days of book printing, spaces were left for initial caps to be drawn in by the few remaining scribes who did that work. As the printing press replaced hand-lettering, the holes were retained as paragraph indentions, and some were filled with decorative type initials.

Decorative settings present mechanical as well as design challenges. Set well, they can be delightful and effective; set poorly, they seem confusing and gratuitous. In your work, you can be as elaborate as you like with initial letters, as long as they fit the text, layout and other constraints. You probably won't find it practical to craft initials by hand, although there are still artists in the world who do this work—even in gold leaf.

Initial caps and drop caps create relief for the eye and provide visual appeal. They're designed either to stick up above the line, or to fit into the text block—a "three-line" or a "seven-line" initial, for example. The keys to success in setting either style are proper alignment between initial letter and text-face baselines; good visual alignment of the initial letter along the left-hand margin; and proper fitting of the text around the initial cap. The process is more complicated with a drop cap than one that rides the base of the first line.

Most initial caps and drop caps create relief for the eye and provide visual appeal. They're designed either to stick up above the line, or to fit into the text block—a "three-line" or a "seven-line" initial, for example. The keys to success in setting either style are proper alignment between initial letter and text-face baselines; good visual alignment of the initial letter along the left-hand margin; and proper fitting of the text around the initial cap. The process is more complicated

Most initial caps and drop caps create relief for the eye and provide visual appeal. They're designed either to stick up above the line, or to fit into the text block—a "three-line" or a "seven-line" initial, for example. The keys to success in setting either style are proper alignment between initial letter and text-face baselines; good visual alignment of the initial letter along the left-hand margin; and proper fitting of the text around the initial cap. The process is more complicated with a drop cap than one that rides the base of the first line.

Large initial letters are usually capitals. But there's no reason why they cannot be lowercase or some variant, such as an ancient script form.

*W**hy not, initial caps and drop caps create relief for the eye and provide visual appeal. They're designed either to stick up above the line, or to fit into the text block—a "three-line" or a "seven-line" initial, for example. The keys to success in setting either style are proper alignment between initial letter and text-face baselines; good visual alignment of the initial letter along the left-hand margin; and proper fitting of the text*

*Y**es, initial caps and drop caps create relief for the eye and provide visual appeal. They're designed either to stick up above the line, or to fit into the text block—a "three-line" or a "seven-line" initial, for example. The keys to success in setting either style are proper alignment between initial letter and text-face baselines; good visual alignment of the initial letter along the left-hand margin; and proper fitting of the text around the*

Some initial caps and drop caps create relief for the eye and provide visual appeal. They're designed either to stick up above the line, or to fit into the text block—a "three-line" or a "seven-line" initial, for example. The keys to success in setting either style are proper alignment between initial letter and text-face baselines; good visual alignment of the initial letter along the left-hand

You can also use a three- or four-line drop cap, enlarged beyond display size, as a column headpiece that reads into and coheres with the text. At these large sizes many individual letters take on interesting shapes not distinguished at text sizes. The resulting white spaces within and around the letters can be pretty interesting, too.

Manipulation Effects

Digital manipulation of type and illustration program capabilities allow extreme special effects that weren't possible in former technologies. Type characters can be enlarged beyond sizes common to layout programs and parts can be cropped out.

Subtle twists, twirls, reverses, unusual letter combinations and even reverbs—such as multiple images with inversions and overlaps—can be worked on those innocent typographic elements to give them a new life as pictures. An illustration program is very useful to the typographer for the tricks it can play on type.

Type Families

And don't overlook the new ideas to be found in bringing distant members of a type family into play as decorative devices. For instance, since the italic of many typefaces is somewhat decorative in itself, it's often a natural for secondary, purely ornamental usage. If you let your imagination loose, you may find yourself way out on the fringes of a type family, where the ultrabold italic lives, hacking and twisting a peculiar-shaped "g" into a stunning graphic surprise.

Ornamental Faces

We have seen that type has evolved through time, that at every significant juncture typefounding has provided us with some advancement of fundamental shape, concept and style. This rich heritage gives the typographer an array of ornamental faces to work with.

The burgeoning of advertising and woodcut letter technology in the last century broadened the scope of decorative typography to include the humorous, the antiquated and the bizarre. Recent technologies such as photo- and transfer-lettering, along with digital techniques, make almost anything possible. If you can dream it up, you can probably design it cheaply and quickly, and you have only yourself to blame for the way it turns out.

Blackletter   Typography.

Script   Typography.

Uncial   typography.

Some of the faces that make good starting points for exploring decorative types are blackletter, from the earliest days of printing; scripts, those fragile and ornate faces with flourishes and frills, based on steel pen handwriting; and uncials, a letterform subgroup that predates printing. These type styles all have solid historical precedents and have withstood the test of time.

*B*ut, these traditional forms give you firm decorative ground from which to launch daring adventures. But at the same time, I must warn you.

*W*hen using ornamental faces it doesn't take much to overstep the boundaries of good design. A few initial letters and a heading or two will create a strong impact, whereas this theory could be stretching.

*T*he idea to every page might look excessive—even boring. Often, more is not better. A few initial letters and a heading or two will create a strong impact, whereas this

ORNAMENTAL

TYPEFACES

Ornamental

Typefaces

These traditional forms give you firm decorative ground from which to launch daring adventures. But at the same time, I must warn you that in using ornamental faces it doesn't take much to overstep the boundaries of good design. A few initial letters and a heading or two will create a strong impact, whereas stretching the idea to every page might look excessive—even boring. Often, more is not better.

It's important to understand the nature of these ornamental faces in order to use them with best results. Blackletter and script faces, for example, were never intended to be used in lines of all capitals. And some of the early woodcut advertising faces are so constrained in shape or so fanciful in design that they're just plain unreadable in extended use, so that a single word or letter here and there is all the printed page can stand.

You can imagine the challenges you might encounter in trying to fit various letter shapes into existing text settings. If the initial is a cap T, then aligning the base is no problem—unless it's a decorative letter with an ornate bottom serif. The margin on the left must be adjusted for the crossbar to hang out into the margin, avoiding an apparent hole. If you're setting into the lines, you must decide whether the configuration of text will follow the shape of the T or remain rectangular; either can be used, depending on the circumstances.

Therefore, you can imagine the challenges you might encounter in trying to fit various letter shapes into existing text settings. If the initial is a cap T, then aligning the base is no problem.

There's a decorative letter with an ornate bottom serif. The margin on the left must be adjusted for the crossbar to hang out into the margin, avoiding an apparent hole. If you're setting into the lines, you must decide

Only if the initial is O, will the rules change. Alignment along the bases must be purely visual; the left-hand margin, the same (you may or may not have to hang over the margin).

ON WHETHER you follow the shape of the initial with the lines of text, that will be dependent on how many lines the initial occupies and how it looks. The larger the initial letter, the more predominant the serif shapes

The initial is T, the rules change. Alignment along the bases must be purely visual; the left-hand margin, the same (you may or may not have to hang over the margin).

And whether you follow the shape of the O with the lines of text will depend on how many lines the initial occupies and how it looks. The larger the initial letter, the more predominant the serif shapes will

If the initial is O, the rules change. Alignment along the bases must be purely visual; the left-hand margin, the same (you may or may not have to hang over the margin). And whether you follow the shape of the O with the lines of text will depend on how many lines the initial occupies and how it looks. The larger the initial letter, the more predominant the serif shapes will be, and they'll be a factor in adjusting along the left margin. T looks better in a rectangular space than A does, because of the shapes. If you plan to use a whole series of initial caps, it's a good idea to list them and maybe rough them out in advance, to create a size and style that will look good with them all.

Some page programs treat drop caps as a style-sheet function, so they can be treated as part of the text; in other programs, you must always place them as separate elements. Placing initial caps "by hand" forces you to position them visually rather than mechanically. This method produces the best effects, even though it's slower and may require minor adjustments as the layout develops.

Remember that if the initial sticks up above the first line, it creates an area of white space that can be effective if you use it positively to help give dynamic tension to a heading.

Finally, it's traditional after an initial cap to set the remaining letters of the first word in small caps. If you decide to use this style, you'll need to be consistent with it.

Also, don't forget that whatever decorative face you choose must be stylistically compatible with the basic text face. Unfortunately, there are no hard-and-fast rules to determine compatibility; sometimes, the unlikeliest typeface combinations treated in the right way can be made to work together in the right circumstances. If you're a beginning designer, you'll develop typographic judgment as you go along, recognize the bloopers when you see them, and click them out.

Dingbats

Now you get to meet the dingbats. The more appropriate and traditional name for these useful typographic additions is "printers' flowers." Nonessential ornaments have been cast along with typefaces since the very early days of printing and, like types, follow a historical progression.

Dingbats have not been left out in the explosion of new inventions, as designers work and play in the digital medium. Dingbats range all the way from simple dots through the marvelous oak leaves and arabesques of the 16th and 17th centuries, to the well-known images in the Zapf Dingbat collection (on many systems) and the whimsies of the new digital designs. Practically any typographic style you care to attempt, from the sedate to the zany, can be found in a set of dingbats on a disk somewhere.

COTTON MATHER

Reserved Memorials (1681 – 1724)

FOR MORE THAN forty years—not daily, but sporadi-
cally—Cotton Mather recorded experiences and thoughts
in a large manuscript that he called his *Reserved Memorials*,
partly intended as a spiritual guide for his pupils and younger
relatives. It was not published until the twentieth century.
Although its modern editor gave it the title of *Diary*, it is
more a series of crafted meditations (often written down well
after the event passed) than spontaneous jottings like those
in Sewall's diary. Despite its craft and care, no work in
Mather's vast production gives a more intimate sense of his
character and mind.

❖

Nonessential decoration has a long tradition in typography and in formal handwriting before that. Set within a text, these
small flowers and other pictures can
provide section and even paragraph breaks
in a short piece; enlarged, they serve as
centerpieces in a layout or "tailpieces" at
the ends of chapters, sections and whole
texts. Often they're used most effectively
to expand or extend the contents of a title
page or display layout, where there's not
quite enough text to fill out the design.

Sometimes they just help make things
pretty—and that's all right, too. The drawings of telephones, pencils, curved arrows,
et cetera, serve the more practical purpose of calling attention to
important particulars—in situations in which the eye might see a
picture yet ignore the words.

While it's possible to use appropriate printers' flowers to allude to
historic periods, dingbats need not be used only in the context of
their periods. It could require some extensive research into specimen sheets and books on type history to discover just when and
where a particular style of flower originated. However, it may be
quite a challenge to place the 1600s among condensed bold sans
faces in a contemporary magazine layout.

Other Graphic Devices

If you could visualize what a printer used to go through to get an
ordinary box rule around a column of type, you would be even more
impressed by how easy it is to create *borders, boxes* and *graphic shapes*
of all kinds using desktop publishing programs. Decorative rules,
various thicknesses of straight lines and combinations of multiple
lines all came on long strips of lead, which had to be cut to length
and mitered with a special tool. Fitting was a nightmare, and any
shape other than a simple rectangle required elaborate measures.

Nevertheless, hundreds of special decorative border rules were designed for typographers, and many of them are still available today. Often ornamental borders were made up of pieces of type, with special characters designed for corners. These were called combination ornaments, and they're also easy to make on the computer with illustration tools. Some are now available as separate characters.

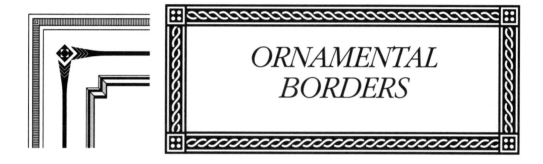

In the past, *screen tints* within borders were also a special problem. Now these effects can be achieved with a couple of keystrokes, along with the other simplified graphics we've looked at. However, screen tints can still be problematic: like photographs, they introduce a tonal complexity—the element of gray—that departs from the pure typographic interrelationship of black shapes and white space. Because of this, type used with screens may need a different treatment (i.e., face, style, size or weight).

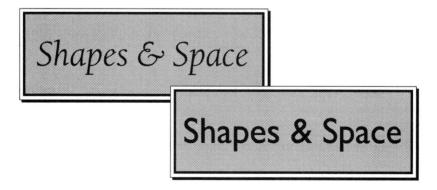

How Much Is Too Much?

The key to effectiveness with all these graphic shapes and devices is restraint. In the early days of desktop publishing, the drop-shadow border was such an accessible graphic gimmick that it appeared everywhere in the medium. I, for one, got really sick of it. When used sparingly, however, a drop-shadow border can enhance an illustration!

In publications, the placement of boxed copy, with or without screens, can be a potent flag to call attention to a particular item. But if there are too many of these, the eye merely passes over them and they lose their punch.

How can you tell? Obviously, one boxed item will really stand out on a page or on the spread of a newsletter. Two or three across a full spread may work, if arranged in an interesting way. But if you begin

Box chaos versus an effective boxed article.

to approach graphic clutter—with too many boxes, headings and ornamentation—your intentions become less clear. It's true that the more complex the material, the more useful these devices may be for accenting, separating and ordering material. But I think that if you consistently try to pare away nonessential typographic effects, complex pages will cohere better.

A border sets off a whole page in a nice way, but notice how a border messes with your margins. A full-page border can look static and lifeless, especially if the margins on either side of the rule are the same. To adjust the balance of border and copy, play with the weight of the border material. For example, multiple lines of varying thickness or a hairline rule combined with decorative elements are ways to adjust the weight and visual impact of borders within set margins.

The key to effectiveness with all these graphic shapes and devices is restraint. In the early days of desktop publishing, the drop-shadow border was such an accessible graphic gimmick that it appeared everywhere in the medium. I, for one, got really sick of it. When used sparingly, however, a drop-shadow border can enhance an illustration!

In publications, the placement of boxed copy, with or without screens, can be a potent flag to call attention to a particular item. But if there are too many of these, the eye merely passes over them and they lose their punch.

How can you tell? Obviously, one boxed item will really stand out on a page or on the spread of a newsletter. Two or three across a full spread may work, if arranged in an interesting way. But if you begin to approach graphic clutter—with too many boxes, headings and ornamentation—your intentions become less clear. It's true that the more complex the material, the more useful these devices may be for accenting, separating and ordering material. But I think that if you consistently try to pare away nonessential typographic effects, complex pages will cohere better.

A border sets off a whole page in a nice way, but notice how a border messes with your margins. A full-page border can look static and lifeless, especially if the margins on either side of the rule are the same. To adjust the balance of border and copy, play with the weight of the border material. For example, multiple lines of varying thickness or a hairline rule combined with decorative elements are ways to adjust the weight and visual impact of borders

The key to effectiveness with all these graphic shapes and devices is restraint. In the early days of desktop publishing, the drop-shadow border was such an accessible graphic gimmick that it appeared everywhere in the medium. I, for one, got really sick of it. When used sparingly, however, a drop-shadow border can enhance an illustration!

In publications, the placement of boxed copy, with or without screens, can be a potent flag to

call attention to a particular item. But if there are too many of these, the eye merely passes over them and they lose their punch.

How can you tell? Obviously, one boxed item will really stand out on a page or on the spread of a newsletter. Two or three across a full spread may work, if arranged in an interesting way. But if you begin to approach graphic clutter— with too many boxes, headings and ornamentation— your intentions be-

come less clear. It's true that the more complex the material, the more useful these devices may be for accenting, separating and ordering material. But I think that if you consistently try to pare away nonessential typographic effects, complex pages will cohere better.

A border sets off a whole page in a nice way, but notice how a border messes with your margins. A full-page border can look static and lifeless, especially if the margins on either side of the rule

Varying the line thickness of borders and adding rules between columns can add visual interest to an otherwise dull page.

Runarounds

Here's where pure typography and illustration meet. (There are other places, such as captions.) Page makeup programs have made the formerly tricky business of running text around an irregularly shaped illustration easy. Imagine how difficult this must have been when both type and pictures were carried on solid rectangular blocks! Now it's merely a command function.

But there are still some hazards. Here's a good example of the tight interaction between design and function: it must not only look great but work great, too.

A primary concern is readability. Running around the right side of a large irregular shape means an uneven left margin, which, for all its visual effectiveness, may lose the reader in a maze of difficult reading. It depends a lot on the nature of the text; small illustrations don't raise the problem.

Here's where pure typography and illustration meet. (There are others, such as captions.) Page make-up programs have made the formerly tricky business of running text around an irregularly shaped illustration easy. Imagine how difficult this must have been when both type and pictures were carried on solid rectangular blocks! Now it's merely a command function.
But there are still some hazards. Here's a good example of the tight interaction between design and function: it must not only look great but work great, too.

Here's where pure typography and illustration meet. (There are others, such as captions.) Page makeup programs have made the formerly tricky business of running text around an irregu-larly shaped illustration easy. Imagine how difficult this must have been when both type and pictures were carried on solid rectangular blocks! Now it's merely a command function.
But there are still some hazards. Here's a good example of the tight interaction between design and function: it must not only look great but work great, too. It's all part of design, A primary concern is readability. Running around the right

Runarounds with uneven left margins can present readibility problems that are avoided by flush-left margins.

Another consideration is the amount of white space that separates these two diverse elements. You need enough separation to prevent competition between illustration and text, but not enough to destroy the coherence of the two elements. Beware of seeing this as only a visual problem, especially at thumbnail size on the screen. Pull proofs, read them, hold them upside down and sideways until a good balance is achieved.

Reverses

Another graphic device readily available on the desktop is type set in reverse field—white type on a black ground. These reversed images work well within ruled borders and as bands across columns for headings. But notice that they won't work as well for ragged settings because of their rigid geometric margins.

rk well	**PHASE 2a**	ages w
·rs and		border
)lumns	**Preparing**	colum
:e that	**to Go:**	that th
vell for	**THE LIST**	for ra§
1use of		of th(
c mar-		margi1
nses of	Another graphic device readily	of the
:k box	available on the desktop is type set	that fr.
·se type	in reverse field—white type on a	within
the ef-	black ground. These reversed im-	can be
1matic.		for the

Avoid reverse overkill.

1 ruled	**PHASE 2a**	reverse
across		within
notice	**Preparing**	bands
as well	**to Go:**	head F
)ecause	**THE LIST**	won't ·
metric		ged set
senses		rigid §
:k box	Another graphic device readily	Then
·se type	available on the desktop is type set	word)
? effect	in reverse field—white type on a	frame:
. So go	black ground. These reversed im-	within
1 other		can be

Restraint is most effective when using reverses.

Wherever you can justify (in both senses of the word) the black box that frames the reverse type within the layout, the effect can be quite dramatic. So go for the drama of it. In other words, don't clutter a reverse image with too much text, or with type that's too small or too delicate to hold up well within the field of black. Sans and bold faces seem to be the best choices for reverses.

Special Type Characters

Exploring your keyboard and the standard character set that usually comes with the typefaces you buy will show you an array of typographic accoutrements. You may not use these often, but they're worth knowing about for the times they'll come in handy.

Ligatures—most commonly fl and fi, but also ff, ffi and ffl in some fonts—help give your text a finished look.

Bullets are useful organizers. They often appear too large set in the same size as the surrounding type, so you can reduce them by a couple of point sizes for a better typographic effect.

Faces are beginning to include many special characters, such as

- decorative—or swash—letters
- ornaments
- other dingbats

Faces are beginning to include many special characters including

- decorative—or swash—letters
- ornaments
- other dingbats

Reduce bullet size by a couple of points to improve the list's appearance.

As font packaging becomes more sophisticated, faces are beginning to include many of the special characters traditionally found in the printer's type cases, such as decorative—or swash—letters, ornaments and other dingbats. As these typographic refinements provide more and more options, the complexity of setting up any job grows. Because of the constraints of the keyboard, you'll find that sometimes it's not worth the time it takes to access all the refinements possible in a given setting. Most desktop publishers use them rarely or not at all.

So, for more efficiency, you should gauge your work in advance to determine what level of finish and precision is required.

Ancillary typographic materials make quite a kit by themselves, and the decorative, the "nonessential," can help create a unique and dynamic typographic style, as long as you keep in mind that the words come first.

Building Your Type Library

Building Your Type Library

I have always called my typographic collection a "type library." Partly, I suppose, because it acts as a reference to pick and choose from, and partly because typographers, like book lovers, are collectors. And while our "library" no longer glows with the mellowness of old maple furniture and letters cast in lead, we still spend a lot of time and thought acquiring it, adding new discoveries and filling out series.

These days, my collection consists of a little box of original disks that act as backup for those in my system and as a storage warehouse for the ones I'm not currently using. As the collection grows, backup disks are added; rarely are types discarded. Why get rid of them if they occupy so little space? So the collection grows in 3 1/2-inch-floppy-disk increments. Now I can carry the entire history of typography, and then some, in a lunch sack.

The goal in establishing a type library is to have available all the faces necessary and desirable for your work. Service bureaus and professional designers try to build collections that cover everything, in order to serve the needs of all clients. In your own case, the collection should be adequate for all current and proposed work, and also allow you to grow and learn.

You also want to get as much use as possible out of a typeface—to maximize your investment and also to see that face in a variety of settings. A type library should provide several possible typeface choices for any particular job, plus a range of companion faces for different effects.

Finally, your type library should be rewarding to use. It should contain faces you enjoy looking at, faces that offer new pleasures in different settings. For me, one of those faces is Caslon. Even in its rather stiff digital renditions, Caslon offers just enough variety in different sizes and versions, so that it constantly appeals to my eye. And it looks so much like antique printing at 300 dpi that I find it very useful for short runs of broadsides and small books.

Other faces will have the same appeal for you, and some may be among those I don't care for. Let your own interests be your guide; let a few mistakes happen. Have a typographic fling now and then—in this medium you have little to lose and a lot to learn.

Augmenting Resident Fonts

Your laser printer's resident fonts will naturally form the core of your collection. But notice how quickly you find they're not getting the workout you'd expect, even though they save all that downloading time. The only resident face I ever use these days, and that rarely, is Palatino. Why is this? I think it's because those resident fonts have not been assembled according to any pattern, but are merely an aggregate of faces that are "popular" according to some mysterious typographic applause meter. They're not put together to interact with one another, they have little historical relevance and they don't even give a very broad range of effects.

For example, Palatino, Century Schoolbook and Bookman are all faces with little contrast between their thick and thin strokes, they all have large x-heights and all set relatively wide, even though they're quite different in style. Yet you can't find a good, solid Old Style face with a small x-height—such as Garamond—or any of the transitional or modern faces, among the resident fonts.

Other writers have proposed a "font slurper" that would remove unwanted resident fonts from printers and allow their replacement with faces of the user's choice. Someday this may be possible. Meanwhile, economy and ease of use dictate that resident fonts form the basis of your collection, and that you build around them to enhance their effectiveness.

Look for faces that provide compatibility or contrast with faces already in your printer. Examples would include acquiring other Zapf faces such as Optima and Michelangelo Titling, when it becomes available, to round out Palatino; and perhaps adding Century Old Style to Century Schoolbook. Build families wherever possible. Faces that extend the visual appeal of Times, especially to use in titles and headings, will make that face considerably more useful.

For some resident faces there's not much help. I cannot see that augmenting Bookman would do much of anything positive, and any attempt would be a wasteful drag on the system. Try it; you'll see.

Text Faces Form the Core

The range of text faces I use in my work isn't particularly broad. I return to the same ones over and over because they seem to reflect my own vision of how a page of type ought to look.

The faces I choose tend to be grouped according to the kinds of work I do, which is not wide-ranging: books, newsletters, correspondence and proposals, and a little bit of display work. I maintain maybe three or four Old Style faces. I often use Baskerville for correspondence and proposals, and rely on the Stone family for much of my newsletter and display work. Added to these is a handful of decorative faces—from a variety of sources—and one face, an uncial, that I've been designing myself.

The Old Style faces I use have varied somewhat according to new releases available, but currently they are Italian Old Style, a Garamond (the version has changed frequently; at the moment it's Slimbach's from Adobe), Janson and Caslon. Because I review typefaces professionally, I try out a lot of different fonts, putting them into real-world situations as I write about them. But those mentioned have remained in my system throughout.

Italian Old Style	Look at the way type developed over the centuries
Slimbach's	Look at the way type developed over the centuries
Janson	Look at the way type developed over the centuries
Caslon	Look at the way type developed over the centuries

You don't need a huge library for most work. The more you use a typeface in differing situations, the more you'll come to understand it and use it gracefully. By limiting the number of text faces and adding secondary display and decorative faces, you can extend your range and provide yourself with a tremendous type resource on a modest budget.

Look at the way type developed over the centuries, from the gentle and graceful tones of its Renaissance origins, through the refinements and increasing contrast of the transitional and modern faces, to the subtle shapes and robust personality of the contemporary. You can bring these features to bear on your pages by acquiring some version of each major stylistic genre. We usually think of these broad changes in type style as historical, but there's no reason you can't approach these visual effects through contemporary examples.

For the early Renaissance effect you can use Sabon; for the later Old Style, where historical precedent might suggest Janson or Caslon, you could instead pick Matthew Carter's Galliard—somewhere between Garamond and Dutch Old Face. Baskerville is Baskerville, and no one has ever expressed that style we know as Transitional in a better way. And Baskerville is such a useful face, you might as well go ahead and buy it. (In my opinion, this face should be resident in all printers.)

Again, Bodoni is Bodoni. Few have come close to the elegance in the extreme contrast of thick and thin strokes as did Giambatista Bodoni in the types we know by his name, although some of Hermann Zapf's designs, such as Melior and International, retain some of that effect. An alternative might be Caledonia.

Times and Century Schoolbook are resident in most printers, and they fill the need for something straightforward, legible and conservative. Palatino, too, is nearly ubiquitous; and in this case, I believe you have a truly inspired typeface at hand. Its universality has made Palatino somewhat cliché in many eyes, but I still find it looks appropriate in many settings and typographic treatments. Other contemporary faces you might consider are the sans faces Futura and Avant Garde (often a resident font), and new designs in the digital medium, such as the very useful Stone family.

Which Supplier? Which Versions?

Purchasing type for desktop publishing systems can be confusing because of the many different versions of a given typeface available from the digital type "foundries" or type manufacturers. And this is not merely a problem for the beginner; it plagues even those who have a comfortable working acquaintance with types and suppliers.

Unfortunately the problem of different versions goes beyond the name and the digital assembly called the font. It gets into areas of ethics when it comes to naming fonts, and it winds up being a problem that relates only to your particular printing output device and the specific nature of the work you do.

For some of the renowned faces such as Garamond and Baskerville, there are as many approaches to the design as there are makers, and since there's no single authority on precisely what makes a true Garamond, each attempt at a new digital interpretation can claim to be the most faithful in spirit to the original. This pirating of typefaces has been going on ever since the earliest days of printing.

Well, you want to credit the designer of a typeface wherever you can, in the same way that writers of books should get their royalties. But a typeface like Garamond can no longer be said to have a designer, since the man's ideas have been replicated, interpreted and falsely attributed over the centuries.

In the case of new original designs, such as Stone, you can buy from the company Stone did the designs for (Adobe Systems); in that way you're acknowledging the designer's role. So in terms of getting as close as possible to the original, you can use original typefaces wherever possible and buy from companies that in some way acknowledge the true origins of a typeface.

But what about cases like Helvetica, a typeface that has been remade under scores of aliases and reproduced in both accurate and inferior versions. How do you know what you're getting?

No matter which approach you take to versions of your favorite faces, the final test is what comes out of the printer. As you'll explore at greater length in the next chapter, in planning your type library you need to keep in mind that some typefaces, and some versions of those typefaces, will look good or bad depending on the device used to create the final image. It's not just that some types look their best only at higher resolutions; it's also the case that types from certain foundries look better on certain printers than on others. Not only that, but different typefaces look best at particular sizes on different printers. It's complicated.

I believe standards will emerge (in fact, they're evolving as I write) to assure font buyers that a typeface will look its best within the constraints of the printer used. No one is served by encrypted subtleties that give one typeface an arbitrary edge in quality over another in a particular page-description language. Conversion programs are available for moving typefaces between page description languages and for maximizing type quality in unusual circumstances.

Type drawing programs allow you to actually adjust many existing fonts to improve their performance on your specific machinery. And there's a growing cadre of independent type artisans who can help you improve font quality where it might be necessary. Service bureaus, in addition to providing high-resolution photo output from your disks, are also a rich source of font information, since they keep in close touch with activity in the trade.

On the other hand, ability, opinion and style are strong factors in digitizing type forms—especially those of the past—as are different technologies for creating outline fonts. Therefore, individual attempts at rendering the same historic face may appear quite different from each other, depending on the printing device and paper surface that are employed.

Wherever it's possible to borrow fonts or get samplers from the makers, it would be helpful to do so. As desktop printers become capable of higher-resolution output, the problems of technical quality in types will diminish, although the aesthetic and ethical problems will remain.

There are bound to be faces in your library that have never quite looked right to you, that gather dust (if that's possible) as did those mistakes many of us made in purchases of hot lead or film strips. But you may find yourself dusting them off as your circumstances, your way of looking at types and the demands of your publications change over time.

Type Organizer

You've seen in the chapter on typeface choices that style in type design tends to roughly parallel its history; that types can be grouped along lines of development in order to get a sense of how they vary and how they might best be used. The following collection of faces is intended to give you a method for looking at type, a collection of specific faces you can put to use immediately, and a basic library on which you can begin to build your own collection. You should be able to adopt or reject faces from the specimens assembled here according to your publication needs, your growing understanding of typographic forms and your own tastes and interests.

Keep in mind that this is my list, and while I've tried not to let my own prejudices interfere, someone else's type collection would be different, and yours will be, too. It's not necessary that these faces be part of your collection; it's possible that none of the faces here will be among the ones you choose. The real intent is to provide a methodology for picking types, and using them, based on their forms and their most obvious functions. This list contains mostly text faces, reflecting their foundational nature in all typography.

Historical

Bembo

Returning to the roots of typography, Bembo is based on a typeface created for one of the greatest printers after Gutenberg, Aldus Manutius of Venice, who printed and published at the turn of the 16th century. The Monotype Corporation in England—pursuing a program of reviving ancient typefaces in the early years of this century—produced Bembo, based on one of Aldus's most beautiful faces. This typeface was cut by the great designer Francesco Griffo, who designed all of Aldus's fonts. Now several versions of Bembo are available in digital form—the best one, I think, from Monotype.

Monotype Bembo has a relatively small x-height and graceful relationships between x-height, ascenders and descenders and capital letters. Traces of pen forms can be seen in the lowercase a, f and r—shapes that were refined out of sight until the revivals of our day. Bembo is extremely legible in small sizes and holds up well to the rigors of low-resolution printing. From that perspective, Bembo is almost an ideal text face. From another point of view, however, the face is almost too complacent. It carries the conceptual refinement and generalized characteristics of the ages, but it has little personality of its own.

On the page, Bembo presents that mellow gray quality of the early roman types, allows for minimal leading, works extremely well in the line lengths used for newsletters and books, but perhaps crowds in too much for the long lines of manuscripts, correspondence and reports. The face mixes well with contrasting display type; if the larger sizes are used for heads they may appear a little too formal. The italic is one of the best available, and can be used for long settings on its own. There's an elegance to these Renaissance types that keeps them from being too comfortable on wildly experimental pages, and Bembo works best in the more sedate designs.

Monotype Bembo has a relatively small x-height and graceful relationships between x-height, ascenders and descenders and capital letters. Traces of pen forms can be seen in the lowercase a, f and r—shapes that were refined out of sight until the revivals of our day. Bembo is extremely legible in small sizes, and holds up well to the rigors of low-resolution printing. From that perspective, Bembo is almost an ideal text face. From another point of view, however, the face is almost too complacent. It carries the conceptual refinement and generalized characteristics of the ages, but it has little personality of its own. ¶ On the page, Bembo presents that mellow gray quality of the early roman types, allows for minimal leading, works extremely well in the line lengths used for newsletters and books, but perhaps crowds in too much for the long lines of manuscripts, correspondence and reports. The face mixes well with contrasting display type; if

Bembo

abcdefghijklmnopqr
stuvwxyzABCDEF
GHIJKLMNOPQR
STUVWXYZ&!?$¢
1 2 3 4 5 6 7 8 9 0 0

Garamond

In the few short decades between the time of Aldus in Italy and Claude Garamond in France, the printing trades had broken off into separate entities instead of all being contained under the same roof. The trend was now toward specialization, as represented by Garamond, the first independent type designer and founder, selling and spreading types to printers all over Europe.

Looking at the way the name Garamond has been used and abused gives you some idea of just how busy the world of printing and publishing has been over these few hundred years: research still goes on trying to figure out which faces were truly his. I like to think of Garamond as an apotheosis, an idea in type design, an ideal of grace, refinement and beauty in letterforms that has been attempted many times, and only occasionally achieved.

The number of versions—metal, photo and now digital, good ones and bad—attests to the importance of the letterforms we call Garamond. Out of them you can see the structure, the idea emerge. Attribution to pen lettering is minimal, although some of the shapes a pen makes when drawing letters have never really disappeared from type. In Garamond the wedge shapes and a certain angularity from former types have become rounded, and some elements to the drawing (or cutting), such as in the cap T and W and the lowercase a and r, are typical type forms, not the forms of hand-lettering.

I'm surprised that I haven't seen laser printers with Garamond installed as a resident font, for it's truly the basic face. It can be used, if no other choices seem better, for virtually any situation, and get by. Used extensively in magazine and book work, Garamond accommodates itself to a wide range of column widths and varying amounts of line spacing. Your business associates won't think you're weird if you use the face, in sizes above 12 point, for correspondence. A ready mixer, Garamond goes with innumerable display faces, especially the sans. And through judicious combinations, you can make this face express virtually any style, from antique to ultra-modern.

GARAMOND

In the few short decades between the time of Aldus in Italy and Claude Garamond in France, the printing trades had broken off into separate entities instead of all being contained under the same roof. The trend was now toward specialization, as represented by Garamond, the first independent type designer and founder, selling and spreading types to printers all over Europe. ¶ Looking at the way the name Garamond has been used and abused gives you some idea of just how busy the world of printing and publishing has been over these few hundred years: research still goes on trying to figure out which faces were truly his. I like to think of Garamond as an apotheosis, an idea in type design, an ideal of grace, refinement and beauty in letterforms that has been attempted many times, and only occasionally achieved. ❦ ❦ ❦ ❦ ❦

Garamond

abcdefghijklmnopqr
stuvwxyzABCDEF
GHIJKLMNOPQR
STUVWXYZ&!?$¢
1 2 3 4 5 6 7 8 9 0

Janson

The interpretation of Garamond's typefaces by artisans of the Netherlands in the 17th century led to a style of letter that remains a standard to this day. The most famous exponent of the "Dutch Old Face" is the one Stanley Morison reworked for the *Times* of London. Other renditions have held a solid place in founders' and printers' catalogs through the decades. One of the best forms, as well as one of the best digital renditions, was originally cut not by a Dutchman but by the Hungarian typographic genius Nikolas Kis, who was working in Holland.

The typeface we know as Janson, with its punches and matrices meandering over the decades amongst the founders' and printers' specimen books, became another generic face, named after a noted Dutch printer who held the types for a time. Only recently was its true origin made known.

Compared to Garamond, Janson produces increased color on the page. Serifs are still those wedges we associate with earlier forms, but there's noticeably more vertical stress in the letters, and more weight in the thick strokes. This is not to say the type is more refined, in the manner that it became refined toward the end of the next century, but this typeface represents a change in the way of looking at type on a page.

Janson and other types based on the Dutch model provide excellent alternatives to Times Roman and other frequently used faces. Because it's such an excellent face for publication work, Janson forms a solid beginning for a typographic library.

Every collection has a small core of legible text faces essential for day-to-day work, and Janson is one of the most sensible choices to fill that need. Compared to Times, Janson supplies the same robust color in a mass of text, but the relationship of x-height to ascending and descending letters is better. Because of this fine balance, there's a more graceful feeling to Janson, and none of the stinginess of more modern faces. The openness of the reading line allows you to get away with little or no leading, especially when the lines are short.

In publications, you want the reader to know that you take your material seriously, that you're not being too flippant. But that doesn't mean you have to be stiff and merely legible over every other consideration. Janson is sober enough for an annual report, yet its homey appeal suits the columns of a company newsletter. The face mixes well with decorative and display types, and does not seem to me to have any noticeable antique or period feeling to it—even though it's an Old Style face—that would limit its usefulness in documents meant for contemporary readers. This seems true of the great types of different historical periods and is probably the reason they tend to endure.

J ANSON and other types based on the Dutch model provide excellent alternatives to Times Roman and other frequently used faces. Because it's such an excellent face for publication work, Janson forms a solid beginning for a typographic library. ¶ Every collection has a small core of legible text faces essential for day-

Janson

abcdefghijklmnop
qrstuvwxyzABCD
EFGHIJKLMNO
PQRSTUVWXYZ
&!?$¢1234567890

Galliard / Granjon

Two other faces that occupy a kind of visual halfway point between the mellow elegance of Garamond and the robust simplicity of Janson are Galliard—a modern interpretation by Matthew Carter— and Granjon—an excellent book face. Granjon was issued by the Linotype Company for composition in metal and the typeface was digitized by Bitstream.

Two other faces that occupy a visual midway point between the mellow elegance of Garamond of Janson are *GALLIARD* and the robust simplicity Galliard—a modern interpretation by Matthew Carter—and Granjon—an excellent book face. Granjon was issued by the Linotype Company for composition in metal and the typeface was digitized by Bitstream.

Galliard

abcdefghijklmnop
qrstuvwxyzABCD
EFGHIJKLMNO
PQRSTUVWXYZ
&!?$¢1234567890

Granjon

Two other faces that occupy a kind of visual halfway point
between the mellow elegance of Garamond and the
robust simplicity of Janson are Galliard
—a modern interpretation by Matthew Carter
—and Granjon—an excellent book face.
Granjon was issued by the Linotype Company
for composition in metal and the
typeface was digitized by
Bitstream.

Granjon

abcdefghijklmnop
qrstuvwxyzABCD
EFGHIJKLMNO
PQRSTUVWXYZ
&!?$¢1234567890

Caslon

My favorite typeface has changed and shifted as I've learned more, become more sophisticated, realized the passions of the moment for the ephemeral things that they were. My Caslon phase has come and gone several times, and when the face first appeared in digital form (not in its best rendition, incidentally) I was hooked again.

Perhaps it should be noted that Caslon is a bit of a love-it-or-leave-it typeface. Some typographers can't abide its quirkiness; others say, "When in doubt, use Caslon."

Caslon Old Face is perhaps our truest connection with an ancient typographic lineage. We see in it the image of early American printing, for it was chosen by Benjamin Franklin for his printing press in the Colonies. It was the face that heralded the typographic revival in England, when printers returned to a more honest page than they were getting from the dispirited "moderns" of the early 19th century. And Caslon comes to us directly: it is still possible to buy the original Caslon, in metal type, taken from the punches and matrices made by William Caslon around 1734. Look for newer, truer versions as they emerge from the various fonteries.

Among the many adjectives writers have used to describe Caslon are "comfortable," "friendly" and "common-sense." These qualities, along with the allusion to American traditions, give you some idea of how you might use this face.

We've all been confronted with a publication that seemed to rebel against every face we could haul out of the library: Times, too chilly; Palatino, too extravagant with space; Helvetica, unreadable! The friendly and comfortable manner of Caslon makes it an ideal choice for those publications that rely on human interest for their effect, such as company newsletters, certain promotional pieces, and book productions of all kinds.

If you're used to putting together publications using hip contemporary types such as Palatino or some of the sans faces, then Caslon is going to appear at first to be too quaint. But I think that as you use the face you'll find the quaintness disappears. For Caslon is truly one of those types that does not obtrude itself upon the eye. Or maybe I should say one that you get used to quickly; your eyes can sail along and absorb the meaning of the words without being distracted by the mechanics of the type. With wide margins and good leading, you could use Caslon in typewriter sizes and larger to good effect in those long reports on 8 1/2 x 11 pages.

The great typographer Robert Grabhorn thought Caslon was at its best in 10 point—in the original, that is. Because descenders are short in many versions, you may be able to go a size smaller in the narrow columns of newsletters. I've always liked the larger sizes—14, 18 and 24, especially 18 point—for poetry books and broadsides.

C ASLON OLD FACE is perhaps our truest connection with an ancient typographic lineage. We see in it the image of early American printing, for it was chosen by Benjamin Franklin for his printing press in the Colonies. It was the face that heralded the typographic revival in England, when printers returned to

But what about the antique quality of Caslon? Does this necessarily date the face, limiting its utility? Set in large sizes, such as in headlines, it's unmistakably Old Style. But try setting uppercase and lowercase in large sizes, flush-left, as you might do with a sans, and see just how robust and up-to-date Old Face can look.

Caslon

abcdefghijklmnop
qrstuvwxyzABCD
EFGHIJKLMNO
PQRSTUVWXYZ
&!?$¢1234567890

Baskerville

Typefaces had been evolving toward a more "refined" form, especially in France, for the 200 years that separate Baskerville from Garamond. But we don't see much evidence of it in historical revivals (the designs didn't last) until the style we call Transitional emerged in England in the middle of the 18th century.

The refinements take the form of a new serif—a thinner horizontal line supported by a graceful "bracket" curving nicely into the main stroke, or stem. Thin strokes are thinner, stress is vertical, and Baskerville sets rather wide compared to its Old Style predecessors. Baskerville himself achieved stunning effects with his typeface using ample leading and letter spacing. And his large sizes—they were different cuttings than the text—have a brilliance we don't see in digital versions. His italic is a radical departure, containing strong hints of the flourished handwriting style of the time (Baskerville himself was a master calligrapher). You can make use of it for some interesting effects.

Baskerville

abcdefghijklmnop
qrstuvwxyzABCD
EFGHIJKLMNO
PQRSTUVWXYZ
&!?$¢1234567890

Baskerville, like Garamond, has found such wide acceptance as a typeface for publications that its absence from resident font collections is surprising. It is so generally readable that it's used as the text face in sober scientific journals as well as upbeat periodicals aimed at a general audience. Baskerville is a good choice in combination with contrasting display, as all the lasting faces seem to be, and there's a personality to it that keeps up a lively interest for the reader.

BASKERVILLE

Typefaces had been evolving toward a more "refined" form, especially in France, for the 200 years that separate Baskerville from Garamond. But we don't see much evidence of it in historical revivals (the designs didn't last) until the style we call "Transitional" emerged in England in the middle of the 18th century. ¶ The refinements take the form of a new serif—a thin horizontal line supported by a graceful "bracket" curving nicely into the main stroke, or stem. Thin strokes are thinner, stress is vertical, and Baskerville sets rather wide compared to its Old Style predecessors. Baskerville himself achieved stunning effects with his typeface using ample leading.

Bodoni

Terminologies can be confusing. Jumping from the Transitional style of John Baskerville of Birmingham, England, to the so-called "modern" faces of Giambatista Bodoni of Parma, Italy, it may appear that there is little consequential connection between the two. Remember that for decades type styles on the continent had been tending toward the forms we call Modern. But our contemporary vision of type styles has pretty much abandoned them.

Caslon marks the waning of the Old Style in a face that has persevered, and Baskerville remains a benchmark of the Transitional style. There are vast reaches of European typography unrepresented in digital form; Bodoni is one of the very few survivors of its kind.

Structurally, Bodoni expresses the antithesis of the Old Style in its strong vertical stress, relentlessly thin horizontal serifs, the astonishing color it can give to a page and its precise but not rigid uniformity. Rather than flowing along the line, the eye tends to distinguish the presence of each letter.

A page set in Bodoni has a unique appearance—it's usually unmistakable. There's a great clarity about those lines of pristine thin serifs and regular upright thick strokes. But in this elegance of precision, there's a coolness never found in Baskerville's printing. And I'd have to say that Bodoni's work, the image of his work that has come down to us, seems to suffer from this over-refinement.

Bodoni lacks the universal utility of Times, Garamond, or even Baskerville. It's just not one of those faces you can use to set almost anything: the tone of your text will be strongly affected by being set in Bodoni. It will take on a formality that you may not wish to convey; and the face is not a good choice for casual communications.

It's not an eminently legible face in small sizes. The master himself continued the *livre de luxe* style that he had learned from Baskerville, incorporating wide margins, large type sizes and generous leading (with virtually no ornamentation) to give his typographic ideas full play on the page.

Try to set your text in the largest point size possible, within reason. You'll soon see how important it is to allow generous leading: without sufficient line space, those pronounced vertical strokes will incline the eye toward reading up and down instead of across. It's also best to restrict decoration to simple rule borders and spare and subtle dingbats.

As an example of a startling variation on Bodoni's themes, look at Bodoni Bold—one of the best display faces you'll find, if you're careful how you combine it with accompanying text. The reason Bodoni Bold is so successful, I think, is because the color is in the vertical strokes, creating an increased contrast with the thins and serifs.

Most bold types show an increase in overall weight; Bodoni combines more weight with greater contrast—with striking results. You can use Bodoni bold and bold italic as decorative elements in themselves: extreme variation in size and weight gives you a lot of black-and-white counters to play with. Widely used for newspaper headlines, Bodoni Bold is a good choice for newsletter display work, combining well with text faces such as Century and some of the sans.

Bodoni has a unique appearance—it's usually unmistakable. There's a great clarity about those lines of pristine thin serifs and regular upright thick strokes. But in this elegance of precision, there's a coolness never found in Baskerville's printing. And I'd have to say that Bodoni's work, the image of his work that has come down to us, seems to suffer from this over-refinement.

Bodoni

a b c d e f g h i j k l m n o p
q r s t u v w x y z A B C D
E F G H I J K L M N O
P Q R S T U V W X Y Z
& ! ? $ ¢ 1 2 3 4 5 6 7 8 9 0

Clarendons / Slab Serif

According to historians, typography and type design went into a long decline during the 19th century. At the same time, the modern machine age—with its steam presses, cheap paper, newspapers, magazines and printed advertising—produced a flood of print never dreamed of in previous centuries, even in the busiest shops. In the interest of visual impact, a plethora of type design ideas resulted.

During these years, all manner of decorative faces and advanced techniques for cutting large letters in wood were born. There was a new way of seeing letters that produced a relatively monotone line.

Use for

short bits

of display

Thus the "Egyptians" were developed, as well as the early sans, or "grotesque," faces—not so much for text but for short hits of display.

I feel that slab serif faces have limited use in text work, but they show up with alarming frequency in the type catalogs, and their typewriter-like monotone lines and generous details do have a place in certain kinds of display settings, and occasionally for headings. The problem with both the Egyptians and the Clarendons in lengthy body copy is that if a weight is used that gives decent color to the page, the letterforms are simply overbearing. If a light face is chosen to resolve the problem, the result is a gray, undifferentiated mass, often boring and unreadable.

Being a "modified Egyptian" with bracketed serifs and a little more modulation of line, the Clarendons are more readable. But I counsel that the whole classification be seen essentially as display, that the faces mix well with many of the roman and sans faces (be critical!), grab attention in all weights and look good in large sizes.

S EPTEMBER

school books

falling leaves

sunny days

Clarendon

abcdefghijklmnop
qrstuvwxyzABCD
EFGHIJKLMNO
PQRSTUVWXYZ
&!?$¢1234567890

Italics

Virtually every roman typeface has an italic that accompanies it; but companion italics were a relatively late addition and were considered a separate face. They were originally used for setting texts in small formats because they saved space; later for major passages in books set in roman; and later still only for setting off quotations, stressed words and foreign phrases. But it's well worth noticing the development of italic typefaces alongside their more visible roman partners, for there's a rich and varied visual resource available to the typographer in the many unusual shapes these ancillary letters have found over the years.

Aldus Manutius developed the first italic typeface in 1501. He based it on a fast clerical hand in current use in the Papal Chancery and among contemporary writing masters. The letters were (and still are) characterized by narrow, evenly sloped letters, and pronounced pen forms, including many kerned letters and ligatures. Aldus used the italic type to set classics in small, inexpensive formats; they still stand as masterworks of the pocket edition. Modern versions of the Aldine italic include Bembo, Blado (the italic accompaniment to Poliphilus, another Aldine revival), Palatino and Stone.

The italics used extensively in French typography departed significantly from the Aldine pen forms. And from then on the subsidiary relationship became firmly established, with italics taking a lesser role as time went on. They demonstrated the same strengthening of thick strokes and refinement of serifs and thins as their roman counterparts do.

It was Kis, the true maker of Janson, who first introduced italics as a functional companion to the roman face. The so-called Janson Italic, and another famous Dutch face, Van Dijck, are excellent italics, and Caslon contains some marvelous swash italic characters. However, when Baskerville, himself a writing master, created the innovative designs for his typefaces, he modeled his italic after the script of the day—with its excess of swirls and flourishes. While muted in the typeface, these hints of popular writing give Baskerville italic a decorative quality that can be very useful in certain settings.

William and Mary
invite you to join them
in the celebration of their marriage.

Saturday, April 12, 1991

The Harcourt Gardens

Janson Italic

abcdefghijklmnop
qrstuvwxyzABCD
EFGHIJKLMNO
PQRSTUVWXYZ
&!?$¢1234567890

Decorative

Blackletter

Typefaces that take their inspiration from the very first types, those of Johannes Gutenberg of Mainz, are called by several names, but "blackletter" seems to be the most descriptive. Blackletter followed its own line of historical development, especially in Germany, where variations of the letterform were used for almost all book printing until early in this century. Some of the great European designers have created stunningly beautiful blackletter faces, and it's too bad that we don't have the visual background to accept this style in books. No other letter can give a page the intensity of color and intricacy of drawing possible with these ancient forms.

Goudy created an excellent and simple blackletter that's available to desktop publishers. And there are others more ornate and not so useful, except perhaps in purely decorative uses.

Blackletter for Emphasis

Blackletter

abcdefghijklmnop
qrstuvwxyzABCD
EFGHIJKLMNO
PQRSTUVWXYZ
&!?$¢1234567890

Uncial

The uncial letter and its brother, the half-uncial, are transitional forms between the all-capital roman inscriptions and the fully developed minuscule, or "lowercase" letter of modern times. We recognize them from the great age of the monastic manuscripts, particularly the famous Book of Kells, a delight to the eye, even in reproductions. From a contemporary typographic standpoint, uncials have limited use, but you should know of them and their potential. Occasionally, they work well for a series of heads that give a certain tone and flavor to a page.

Uncials also have possibilities for announcements, flyers, broadsides and other short texts. Of the uncials available, Victor Hammer's American Uncial is perhaps the most noble, with an accompanying cap font that significantly extends the potential of this beautiful face.

Libra, designed by S. H. de Roos, has a freshness that keeps it looking current 50 years after its making, and it still brightens pages, from serious books to cheerful ephemera. Libra was a favorite of the great book designer Adrian Wilson, who could make it dance.

celebrate with joy

Uncial

abcdefghijklmn
opqrstuvwxyz
&!?$1234567890

Script

When you start looking at script faces, you'll be surprised at how many there are, considering their somewhat limited utility. Scripts are essentially pen forms that come from the era when, with the development of the steel nib, penmanship rose to the height of fashion. From our early school days, many of us remember learning this writing style, with its connected lines, flowing shapes, variations made in the lines from pen pressure, and a lot of flourishes. Scripts are closely allied to italics, but italic type takes its form from the broad pen; italics have a completely different flavor because of the heritage of a different pen.

Be careful with scripts. They can be totally illegible if not used with restraint. There are also good and bad ones, as you'll discover in your explorations. Why some have survived, I don't know, but the digitizers seem determined to reproduce every face ever made, so you can certainly take your pick.

While the flourished shapes might work well for something formal like wedding announcements, some other form based on writing tools—such as brushes or speedball pens—might be more appropriate for heads where a casual look is desired. Be sure to use ample leading, and don't run flourished caps together. Remember, if you can't read it, no one else can either.

Regency Script

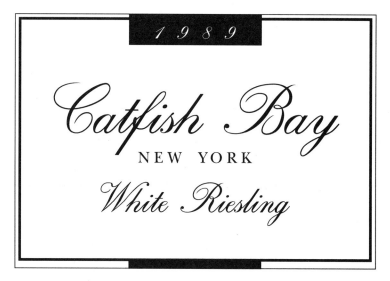

Poster

Faces that come from the wood type era of the 19th century, and designs in that mode that came later, have a definite place in a typographer's collection. But they're used rarely, mostly for special effects, and shouldn't occupy a large part of the library. Here's a situation where finding types in inexpensive packages, perhaps from lesser-known makers, could build a collection of interesting possibilities for very little money.

In addition to the Western themes found among these faces, look at Ritz, Broadway and other faces reflective of the Roaring Twenties. Faces like Italia or Jenson, peculiarities out of the typographic revival, give hints of Art Nouveau. And there are others that may speak clearly of periods or places.

Ritz Laser

The Types of Frederic W. Goudy

Entire books have been written by and about this prolific and influential American type designer. So if you find yourself attracted to Frederic Goudy's designs you may want to know more about his interesting life and ideas. There are other designers, such as Morris Benton, Eric Gill, Hermann Zapf and Jan Van Krimpen, whose work may warrant whole sections, chapters or books. But as desktop publishers, we find Goudy's types increasingly important as a creative resource; and the sheer number of very useful Goudy faces entering the digital medium makes his work important to mention here.

Goudy began designing typefaces in the mid-1890s, during the typographic revival in England and America, and he continued a prodigious career until his death in 1947. Many of his designs were done for the Lanston Monotype Corporation and are currently being reissued by Giampa of Vancouver, B.C. Others were private commissions; many were the products of Goudy's own foundry. Probably the best-known face is Goudy Old Style, available from most suppliers. It's an excellent face for promotional work of all kinds—catalogs, printed advertising, etc.—and contains one of the best bold faces ever produced. Berkeley (originally Californian, designed as a proprietary face for the University of California Press), Kennerly and Goudy Modern are book faces that together provide a range of tone and color on the page that should fit many needs.

Judith Sutcliffe has recreated one of Goudy's more unusual faces, Goudy New Style, used by the Grabhorn Press for its famous edition of *Leaves of Grass* in 1934. His Italian Old Style, an old flame of mine; Garamont; various titling fonts—Hadriano and Lombardic Initials; and his excellent blackletter help to round out this impressive list of typographic resources.

Goudy's types have flair and personality. And while there are almost always a few quirks to be found in the faces because of this, the personality gives his types a liveliness on the page matched only by true stylists such as Zapf. If applied with the same vigor, and if the right face is used for the job, Goudy types can give a series of publications a whole stylistic bent that could be very rewarding to the exploring designer.

Goudy
Old Style

abcdefghijklmnop
qrstuvwxyzABCD
EFGHIJKLMNO
PQRSTUVWXYZ
&!?$¢1234567890

abcdefghijklmnop
qrstuvwxyzABCD
EFGHIJKLMNO
PQRSTUVWXYZ
&!?$¢1234567890

Goudy
New Style

Resident Fonts

Times

The Times New Roman is not quite a revival of a typeface, nor is it really a new design. It was created in 1931 by Stanley Morison, Typographic Director at the Monotype Corporation of England, to fulfill a specific purpose. Morison, and his drawing office, reworked a sturdy Dutch face known as Plantin to meet the visual and technical needs of a mighty newspaper, the *Times* of London.

The idea was in Morison's words "proportion and legibility"—and a new look for the *Times*, whose typographic resources Morison considered "degraded." Legibility in small sizes, proportions suitable for setting in columns and resistance to the exigencies of newsprint production from cylinder stereotypes were all challenges worthy of the intellectual and technical acumen of one of the giants of modern typography.

The result, a "modernized old face," has sharp, generous serifs, a rather narrow set and large x-height, and open interior spaces created by a very careful modulation between thick and thin strokes. To achieve a large, narrow body and still retain shapely serifs and extruding letters is a tribute to the coherence of Morison's design ideas. That Times was one of the first faces to be placed in the fledgling laser printers of the Eighties also attests not only to its legibility in the most adverse conditions, but to its immense popularity in the typographic community as well.

But if a face is redrawn from an existing design, it can be perfected to the point of sterility, since there's none of the fiery impulse of original creation at work. Times suffers from glacial uniformity, dreary repetition of ideal shapes, and uninspired sturdiness. Compare it to Janson, to get an idea of how much can be said in subtle ways. Times works best where the text is just as serious as the typeface.

Legal stuff cries out for Times. Situations in which legibility is at risk—for reasons of type size, printing conditions or specialized readers—may be best approached with this face. And if you're in doubt, Times is safe.

Proportion & Legibility

. . . .

The Times New Roman is not quite a revival of a typeface, nor is it really a new design. It was created in 1931 by Stanley Morison, Typographic Director at the Monotype Corporation of England, to fulfill a specific purpose. Morison, and his drawing office, reworked a sturdy Dutch face known as Plantin to meet the visual and technical needs of a mighty newspaper, the *Times* of London.

The idea was in Morison's words "proportion and legibility"—and a new look for the *Times*, whose typographic resources Morison considered "degraded." Legibility in small sizes, proportions suitable for setting in columns and resistance to the exigencies of newsprint production.

Times New
Roman

abcdefghijklmnop
qrstuvwxyzABCD
EFGHIJKLMNO
PQRSTUVWXYZ
&!?$¢1234567890

Helvetica

Popularity among typefaces is driven by many forces, including high-powered advertising and availability to a broad spectrum of users. In the case of Helvetica, the early decisions by manufacturers to place this face, along with Times Roman, into printers as resident fonts is certainly a primary factor.

Helvetica was designed in 1957 by Max Meidinger. As one of a long lineage of European sans faces, it has enjoyed phenomenal success in all typesetting technologies. Readily available on both sides of the Atlantic, its use has been extended considerably in desktop publishing by its large library of variants.

Helvetica succeeds, I think, because of its unobtrusive legibility. The large x-height gives it a certain authority in heads and other display work; the stronger weights are generally successful.

But if you ignore its ubiquitous presence and its fame, and look dispassionately at the forms of its letters, especially in some of the mutations recently offered, you may well agree with me that the face contains some of the ugliest shapes ever constructed in type. Why, when there are so many well-made sans faces available, you should want to set up even a headline, much less a block of text, in something as ill-proportioned and drab as Helvetica, is a question to ponder seriously. I was not sorry to see the end of those days when all the desktop publishing we saw was set in Times for the text and Helvetica for the heads.

H·E·L·V·E·T·I·C·A

HELVETICA WAS DESIGNED IN 1957 BY MAX MEIDINGER. As one of a long lineage of European sans faces, it has enjoyed phenomenal success in all typesetting technologies. Readily available on both sides of the Atlantic, its use has been extended considerably in desktop publishing by its large library of variants.

Helvetica succeeds, I think, because of its unobtrusive legibility. The large x-height gives it a certain authority in titles, heads and other display work; the stronger weights are generally quite successful.

Helvetica

abcdefghijklmnop
qrstuvwxyzABCD
EFGHIJKLMNO
PQRSTUVWXYZ
&!?$¢1234567890

Palatino

I have been consistently amazed at the fonts chosen as residents in desktop printers. Apparently there's an idea that the most popular faces will be the most useful all ganged together. But even that notion doesn't seem to be consistently followed. However, the inclusion of the extremely popular Palatino on virtually every printer is a piece of sound judgment we can be thankful for.

Hermann Zapf designed Palatino in 1950, and it rapidly became one of the most used types in the world. The face was made for hand composition, machine typesetting in metal (German and American Linotype) and photo composition. Alas, some of the versions departed quite a bit from the clarity and brilliance of the original. Zapf participated in the digitization of Palatino for Linotype (Adobe) and Bitstream, helping to restore the face to its original spirit. Thus, one of the great faces comes to the desktop medium reviewed by its designer and brought to the form in the condition he would like to see it. Be aware that many resident versions are not up to Zapf's standards.

The genius of Palatino is in its treatment of calligraphic shapes as a contemporary medium. Throughout the alphabets, in both the uppercase and lowercase, there is evidence of the hand at work. Pen shapes are elaborated with a care, facility and grace that give the idea of lettering a new life.

Forty years have passed since Palatino was introduced, yet the face seems as fresh as current drawings in the digital medium. And Palatino has been used for every conceivable typographic task, noble and profane, yet it has not become a cliché.

Despite its wide set, the proportions of Palatino make it function well in the narrow columns of newsletters as well as the pages of books in most formats. It needs leading, however, and will stand quite a bit of it. If the lines tend to be long, add more leading till you think it won't bear anymore. Then you'll see how open the lines can be and still hold up. Be careful mixing Palatino, as it won't tolerate rigid companion faces; it's often best kept in its own family, using italics, bolds and large sizes.

Hermann Zapf designed Palatino in 1950, and it rapidly became one of the most used types in the world. The face was made for hand composition, machine typesetting in metal (German and American Linotype) and photo composition. Alas, some of the versions departed quite a bit from the clarity and brilliance of the original. Zapf participated in the digitization of Palatino, for Linotype (Adobe) and Bitstream, helping to restore the face to its original spirit. Thus, one of the great faces comes to the desktop medium reviewed by its designer and brought to the form in the condition he would like to see it. Be aware that many resident versions are not up to Zapf's standards.

The genius of Palatino is in its treatment of calligraphic shapes as a contemporary medium. Throughout the alphabets, in both the uppercase and lowercase, there is evidence of the hand at work. Pen shapes are elaborated with a care, facility

Palatino

abcdefghijklmnop
qrstuvwxyzABCD
EFGHIJKLMNO
PQRSTUVWXYZ
&!?$¢1234567890

Contemporary

The Stone Family

The Stone family was designed by Sumner Stone at Adobe Systems for the specific output resources available to the personal computer user—the 300-dpi laser printer, the high-resolution Linotronic and similar typesetters and everything in between. I have found that Stone works well at all different levels of output.

To design a type capable of setting every kind of text—from the finest book to the sleaziest ad—and at all resolutions is to attempt a universality achieved only by great types such as Baskerville or Palatino. To meet the demands of myriad graphic situations, typefaces are often designed as "families" (that is, types that look like they belong together but have a variety of different shapes).

The concept of a family of types goes all the way back to Nicolas Kis, whose types we know as Janson. Kis cut relative weights for different sizes and introduced the first companion italic. Univers, with its many weighted and sloped variations, neatly numbered according to a grid, extends the family but only within the tight constraints of a contemporary sans-serif. Optima, incidentally, achieves popularity with a basic family of only four variations. Stone has a family of 18.

Responding to the complex structure of many modern documents and publications, Stone broadens the idea of a family to include a sans-serif and—an innovative concept—an "informal" typeface to go along with the roman and italic. Three weights of each provide diversity within an integrated series.

Notice how large the type is on its body: the non-extruding letters are fully half the size of the type overall. This is not as large an x-height as Times, but it's still quite generous (compare it to Garamond, for example). A large x-height means that a typeface will remain readable when set in small sizes. For example, 10-point Stone has the apparent size of many faces set several point sizes larger. But careful spacing is important on shorter lines to avoid having to use additional leading. Large x-height definitely provides economy of space, since it aids legibility where the smaller sizes in laser printing often blur.

The Stone family provides a kind of safety net for the nonprofessional and for the beginning typographer. Stone's underlying continuity makes it easier for the user to put together an attractive layout on the screen. In this respect, the type is also an excellent teaching tool. The esoteric considerations in choosing a typeface can be avoided for the moment and the focus of decision-making put on the more immediate critical questions of size, spacing, roman versus sans, where to use italic and so on.

Later, with expanded knowledge of the history and æsthetics of type design and the increased confidence of experience, other periods and approaches can be included in the type library.

STONE

A Typeface Designed for
Personal Computer Users & Desktop Publishing

Stone Serif

abcdefghijklmnop
qrstuvwxyzABCD
EFGHIJKLMNO
PQRSTUVWXYZ
&!?$¢1234567890

Sans-Serif

Gill Sans

For desktop publishers accustomed to their resident Helvetica and Avant Garde sans-serif faces, it may come as a welcome surprise to discover there are interesting and effective alternatives to these "geometric" models of contemporary style. Rather than relying almost solely on simple curves and straight lines, Gill Sans adheres to the spirit of the noble tradition of roman letterforms; that is, Gill's letters are drawn the way roman letters would be drawn but without the finishing strokes.

The sans-serif series that Gill designed for the Monotype Corporation, starting about 1926, was an attempt to create a letter that could be used in virtually every typographic circumstance—in this case, for a railway system operating throughout England. Thus, the design had to be suited to the tiny footnotes on printed schedules, as well as large compelling signage in the stations.

Edward Johnston, the "father" of modern calligraphy, had tried a similar project a dozen years before, and his designs for the London Underground Railway served to inspire Gill to develop a truly readable sans letter. Between the two attempts, sans-serif type gained stature and a beauty that set standards for sans faces to come.

Gill's type demonstrates how the ideals of good form, grace and simplicity can be achieved even within the context of timetables, signage and advertising for a railway line. Where later sans types reflected the mechanistic, Gill Sans insists upon the humane, denying the necessity of sacrificing humanness to the regular, the repetitive, the bureaucratic.

In use, Gill Sans will give your pages a different quality than they would have set in another sans type. Compare a column set in Helvetica with the same thing set in Gill, and notice how the Gill fits together more like something you'd expect to read, rather than clustering in the small chunks of advertising or display. Although Gill apparently did not see his type primarily as a book face, it works better in text settings than many of the sans faces currently used for that purpose.

Notice how the relation of x-height to overall size is carefully balanced; the typeface actually looks like lettering. Compare this to a face like Helvetica, in which the tyranny of straight line and curve and the overly large body have severely altered the natural flow we've grown to expect from serif letters.

The roman tradition is obvious in certain letters of Gill's face: the a, g, r and t are really roman letters without serifs. But notice, too, that where many sans faces would jam verticals together in an illegible thicket, the Gill maintains the sense of internal space that would be allowed if serifs were attached. This combination of shapely letters and internal space create the deliberate relation of parts necessary in text setting.

At first glance most sans types appear to be made up of monotone lines, yet this is rarely the case. In fact, in order to appear as lines of a single width, the drawings must be subtly altered to accommodate the eye's tendency to group and resolve shapes, making them appear thicker or thinner depending on their juxtapositions with other elements in the drawing. If you examine the sequence of letters closely in Gill Sans, you'll see just how delicately varied and modulated some of these lines have to be to give this type the grace that belies its simplicity.

GILL SANS

Gill Sans

abcdefghijklmnop
qrstuvwxyzABCD
EFGHIJKLMNO
PQRSTUVWXYZ
&!?$¢1234567890

Futura

Futura, designed contemporaneously with Gill Sans, carries forward
the spirit of the machine extolled as a virtue rather than humanism
confronted by the machine. Created by Paul Renner in 1927, Futura
has stood for decades as a kind of resolution of Bauhaus ideas,
carrying to later generations something of the vision of that artistic
movement. There's a precision to the straight lines and perfect
circles of Futura that was somewhat tempered in the slightly more
modeled shapes of later sans faces, such as Helvetica and Univers.
But the model is here; and for purity of form and uncompromised
detail, Futura remains the exemplar.

In the light and book weights, Futura has clarity. Where it lacks
emotion (see Gill) or grace (see Optima), it offers precision, which
in itself can be a provocative graphic idea. There's a coolness here
that fits perfectly with certain kinds of texts, especially where the
typography is not dense and you can manipulate tone and color by
using subtle variations in weight. If you want to play with shapes on
the page, Futura gives you a pallet of grays to paint with.

Where the face fails is in the bolds, particularly the bold condensed.
They adopt an ungainly fatness rather than the shapelier fullness
you can see in later sans designs. To me, these bolds are too reminiscent of ugly newspaper heads, bureaucratic signage and dreary job
printing. Try mixing bolds from other fonts with the lighter weights
of Futura, or use Futura bolds sparingly.

Futura

abcdefghijklmnopqrstuvwxyz
ABCDEFHIIJKLMNOPQRSTU
VWXYZ &!?$¢1234567890

SOUPS

French Onion Soup

$2.95

Soup Du Jour

$2.85

SALADS

Chef Salad

$4.95

Spinach Salad

$4.50

Chicken Salad

$5.25

BURGERS

Standard Burger

$4.95

Cheese Burger

$5.25

Onion Burger

$4.95

Optima

I have the feeling that if only one typeface survives from this hectic 20th century, so filled with new designs and lettering ideas, it will be Optima. Designed by Hermann Zapf in 1958, Optima is heading into its fourth decade of virtually universal application in Europe and America. Created in all typesetting media, Optima was the only notable typeface, besides Helvetica, to become a successful typewriter font—on the IBM Selectric Composer. I can remember the heft and intriguing surfaces of the Stempel Foundry's Optima when it was cast in metal.

So what makes Optima great? I feel a little silly saying this, but I think it's in part because Optima is a serif and a sans-serif type at the same time. Drawing on the spirit of some remarkable lettering by the 15th century Italian sculptor Luca della Robbia, Zapf created flared vertical strokes and other terminals and calligraphic curved shapes and bowls, which give Optima both grace and tremendous energy. The capitals look inscriptional, while the lowercase is briskly typographic. The swelled "serifs" allow a large x-height that does not seem to crowd the terminals of ascenders and descenders. The shapely lines, slightly heftier terminals and well-drawn curves make Optima very legible in small sizes; the bold retains the same modeling and is very successful. And try mixing Optima heads with Palatino text.

Optima is not an ideal laser printer face, however, because lower resolutions won't reproduce the subtlety of line necessary to make the face look good. In its digital issue, Adobe has included a low-resolution version for 300-dpi printing. This is fine for proofing and to my eye is still definitely better than most sans faces. But to be seen at its best, Optima should be produced on an image setter. Look to Stone Sans, a face that owes a stylistic debt to Optima, for a face to work more comfortably at 300 dpi. A good test of improvements in resolution on plain-paper copiers will be their ability to reproduce Optima properly.

Wherever your work calls for this graceful clarity, with classical overtones, where you can make full use of the subtleties that seem so comfortable and involving to the reader—in short, where you want a serif and a sans at the same time—you can rely on Optima to raise almost any text to a slightly heightened level of visual expression.

OPTIMA

LOOK FOR THE DETAILS

I have the feeling that if only one typeface survives from this hectic 20th century, so filled with new designs and lettering ideas, it will be Optima. Designed by Hermann Zapf in 1958, Optima is heading into its fourth decade of virtually universal application in Europe and America. Created in all typesetting media, Optima was the only notable typeface, besides Helvetica, to become a successful typewriter font—on the IBM Selectric Composer. I can remember the heft and intriguing surfaces of the Stempel Foundry's Optima when it was cast in metal.

So what makes Optima great? I feel a little silly saying this, but I think it's in part because Optima is a serif and a sans-serif type at the same time, drawing on the spirit. of some remarkable lettering by the 15th century Italian sculptor Luca della Robbia, Zapf created flared vertical strokes and other terminals and calligraphic curved shapes and bowls, which give

Optima

abcdefghijklmnop
qrstuvwxyzABCD
EFGHIJKLMNO
PQRSTUVWXYZ
&!?$¢1234567890

How to Look at Typefaces

This gathering of typefaces has given you an overview of the historical development and stylistic variations that can form a basic library, upon which you can build any number of variations to suit your own taste and ideas about what looks good. But there are thousands of type designs not shown here; in fact, whole areas of stylistic endeavor in typefaces haven't been shown or discussed. Since all those faces are based on the same alphabet, certain elements are common to them all, and the ways those elements are treated provide clues to their universal structure.

So here are some common anatomical details that will help you identify and categorize typefaces and get to know them better.

Serif shape at head: The shape of the serif leading into the vertical parts of letters gives an excellent clue as to the style of type, its origin and the general tone you can expect from it on the page. In fact, much of the history of type design is the history of the serif. For now, consider the distinct differences in serif shape: thin, horizontal lines; straight lines with "brackets" supporting them like shelves; and triangular wedges—some shapely, some grotesque.

Serif shape at foot: Often the serifs at the feet of vertical strokes and at the tail of the a and the t, while not so distinctive as those at the head, give clues about the workability of a face in setting. These foot serifs help to balance letters in relation to one another.

Shape of arch: Every arched letter, such as m, n or h, springs from its upright at a certain angle and with a particular curve. These characteristics are basic to the way a typeface will look in mass on the page. Look closely at the interior shape created by the arch of an n, for example, and notice how rounded, how wide and how well balanced that white space is. There's a subtle similarity between the arches of typography and the arches of architecture that you might find rewarding to explore.

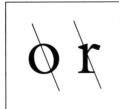

Bowl (counter): While thinking about white space, notice the bowls of letters such as a, g, d or b. As soon as you can begin seeing the white within the black letterform, much of the character of any given typeface will begin to emerge. Bowls have only a loose relationship to arches, and a good type design has to bring these similar but distinct shapes into accord.

Angle of strokes, or bias: The quickest way to notice how the angle of strokes works in an alphabet is to look at the lowercase o. You'll notice that in many cases the shape of the white space in the o mirrors the angle of the line of the serifs. This angularity of stroke, or bias, expresses the heritage of formal penmanship still lurking in many roman alphabets. Formal writing is done with a chisel-shaped pen held at approximately a 30 to 45 degree angle; the movement of the pen creates modulations of thick to thin strokes.

Contrast & modulation: Following on the angle of thick and thin strokes is the way in which the thick shapes move into thin ones. In early types, there was little contrast between thick and thin, and the movement from one to the other was gradual— thick gently curving to thin. What we generally call "modern" faces, on the other hand, express a more extreme and abrupt contrast between thick and thin strokes. The effect on the appearance of a page is pronounced. This is one of the first distinctions you'll need to make in choosing a typeface for a project.

Join of arch and bowl to stem: Look at the lowercase b and d, and at any one of the arched letters (such as h). The way bowls and arches join upright stems helps define certain qualities in the drawing, such as the little foot at the bottom of b and d, in some faces; or, in some alphabets, the shapely modeling where curves join stems.

Modeling of stems: The uprights themselves can be either perfectly straight, curving simply into the serifs, or they can be shaped into graceful curves. The most notable treatment of these carefully modeled stems is in the Optima typeface, in which the curves actually swell to suggest serifs, creating a unique and elegant effect. Desktop printers don't tend to re-produce these modeled stems very well, so it's important to notice them in choosing type.

Lowercase a : The lowercase a is a good identifier for most typefaces; and there are several key places where the character of the face is expressed. The first thing I look at is the free-standing arc at the very head of the letter, which includes a kind of serif that isn't repeated exactly in any other letter of the alphabet. It's the place where the designer seems to instill much of the personality of the face. You'll see either a chisel edge, a blob or—in more modern faces such as Palatino and Stone—a more graceful and shapely cutting. Other key points are where the bowl curves into the upright stroke and the shape of the bowl as this curve defines it. The italic a has a closed bowl; the shape of the top of the italic a is also a signifi-cant point of identification. You can learn a lot from looking at lowercase a's.

Size and shape of capitals: The lowercase alphabet gets the most play in modern typography, so get to know it first. But the appearance of the caps is important, too, and can have a strong effect on a page of text. One important consideration is the relationship of cap size to the lowercase; if caps are too large and imposing, they'll stick out unpleasantly in the text. Many faces, including Bembo, have a capital that is just slightly lower than the lowercase ascenders. This seems to create an ex-cellent balance of color.

Certain capitals, too, have such a commanding appearance that they're part of the personality of the face. The great type designer and artist Eric Gill once said that the cap R was the most significant letter in the entire alphabet, and in some designs you can get a sense of the face from the R alone. Other caps that help in identification are the A, the T and the W.

Overall weight and color: Types can be light, or they can be heavy-handed. Every typeface exhibits a certain "color" on the page. This can be important in trying to give a certain tone to a printed piece. The pronounced difference between Garamond and Bodoni is an extreme example, but color can be increased by overall weight as well as by contrast. For example, compare Garamond and Bodoni to Palatino, or notice the different weights of a slab-serif face like Memphis to see how color is added.

The pronounced difference between Garamond and Bodoni is an extreme example, but color can be increased by overall weight as well as by contrast. For example, compare Gara-	The pronounced difference between Garamond and Bodoni is an extreme example, but color can be increased by overall weight as well as by contrast. For example, compare Gara-	The pronounced difference between Garamond and Bodoni is an extreme example, but color can be increased by overall weight as well as by contrast. For example, com-	The pronounced difference between Garamond and Bodoni is an extreme example, but color can be increased by overall weight as well as by contrast. For
Garamond	Bodoni	Palatino	Memphis

Tails and ears, etc.: There are several free shapes occurring throughout the alphabet that relate strongly to the geometry of the whole but only appear once as a particular form. Look at the head of the f, the apex of the t, the ear on the g, the tail of the y and the shape of the s. These unique elements seem to be where the designer has fun—and sometimes gets carried away to the point of overdoing things a little. If these random shapes contain too many peculiarities, the typeface will look quirky in the setting and be distracting to the reader. Cute is not necessarily readable.

Other stylistic variations can be found within the letters of any typeface, and as you become familiar with more faces, you'll see other more subtle distinctions. But even superficially, the complexity of forms drawn out of the simple geometry of line, angle and curve is pretty astonishing. For me, this is the real fascination of type, and the unending variety of letters ought to help make your work interesting, too.

Design
Considerations

Design Considerations

You've looked at all the basic typographic elements and the way they're assembled—how letter shapes come together on a white field to make a coherent and effective page. And we've talked in terms of the traditions and the "rules" of typography, concepts that apply to all pages in general.

Now it's time to consider the way you think when you design pages, and the steps you take in getting your designs to come together.

It's easy to confuse design with decoration, and that's a mistake, because it is really design as a mental activity—i.e., design as a verb—that makes a thing beautiful, not the finishing touches "pasted on" afterward.

One of my teachers along the way said that a successful work of art (or design) is one in which "the details of its construction are obscured." The design process should smooth the seams and hide the thinking process.

All works of art are designed; anything that's *made* is designed. Design is the mental process by which ideas become objects. A well-designed chair may or may not be a work of art, but every chair that is a work of art is well designed.

In typographic design the objects are printed pages or words on screens. The final product is arrived at through a series of steps. It's partly a process of logic, akin to the "critical path" planning method by which essential procedures are structured out of a complex of possible ones. But there's also a lot of trial and error involved.

The artist creates form and context; the typographer merely assembles and manipulates. On the printed page, typographical design can be seen more clearly because type is arranged, not created on the spot. The pieces are moved around till they look right, not thrown down spontaneously and forever the way a calligrapher lays down ink. This approach may seem mechanistic and not very elegant, but you'd be surprised how satisfying a well-planned project can be, and how much more beautiful the finished product, when the design has been thought through effectively.

To achieve good-looking pages, what principles or aesthetic judgments do you apply? This chapter focuses on universal principles of design and beauty as they relate and apply to type.

The following review of design principles is neither complete nor prescriptive. These explorations can go as deep as you're willing to take them—into the ageless mysteries of why things are beautiful. Here I merely want to recall some of the basic concepts covered in previous chapters, seen from the reader's subconscious aesthetic perspective.

It's also worth mentioning that much of our judgment about the "rightness" of a piece of typography comes from what we don't see. Good typography eliminates the obstacles to pleasurable reading—whether it's a company newsletter, a novel or an advertisement for toilet bowl cleaner. And if it works, we rarely stop and notice how effective the typography is.

Logical Flow/Continuity

It's hard to find a better word than "logical." It seems to me the first goal of typography is to present a piece of writing in such a way that all the parts follow naturally, inevitably and coherently through the levels of its organization. That logic and continuity are what Edward

Johnston called "general uniformity of flow." Typography is the final step in making writing make perfect sense. Bad typography can destroy the good sense of a piece of writing by making it visually incoherent.

Typography should help the reader by establishing a logical flow.

This does not necessarily mean stiff, formal, mechanistic or boring. But the reader is more engaged and attentive when a sense of direction is clear. If you can help the reader quickly find the thread of your presentation and follow it, then maybe it won't get dropped in the trash or have the page turned.

Balance/Dynamic Harmony

Balance is not stasis. In fact, stasis is to be avoided; it makes the reader nervous. More print has been ignored because it had no visual tension on the page than for any other reason. That's my opinion. In the beginning, we discussed arranging margins to make them dynamic on the page, and we've kept up the rap about the tough interaction between black and white elements.

In all good typographic arrangements, through adjustments in size, style and placement, the parts find a harmonious relationship with one another that seems natural and appropriate to the content. You can see it if you squint and just keep fixing things until that balance emerges.

Avoid stagnant pages and strive to achieve balance and interest.

Simplicity

It's easy to talk about the value of simplicity, but it's an aesthetic principle that's remarkably difficult to achieve. Editors cut, cut, cut—or they should. But once the text is final, simplicity must be maintained through typographic arrangement and restraint in developing interesting effects.

Some projects are complicated! How do you go about keeping a newsletter simple when it's jammed with different stories, photos, sidebars and elements that can sometimes clutter up the page? How do you find the underlying simplicity in a complex sequence or arrangement of ideas?

This is where your understanding of the intent of the text and attention to information hierarchies can be so important. If you can see the primary purpose of a publication clearly, then it's easier to strip away confusing or extraneous digressions. Even if the type wants to be scattered all over the page, a scattering of faces should maintain an underlying order.

Poor hierarchy.

Good hierarchy.

As possible solutions to any typographic problem develop, they should conform to the overall purpose. One of the hardest things to do in any creative endeavor is to throw out good ideas. The scrapbook in my Mac is filled with ideas I couldn't stand to give up; I no longer even remember why some of them were so good.

So you see that the restraint of simplicity is not simple-mindedness but elegance and respect for the reader. This is really a pretty tough discipline. But you'll be remembered for it.

Consistency

In classical aesthetics, the concept of *unity* is fundamental. As my dictionary puts it, unity means "singleness of design or effect, or the coherence of parts into a whole thing." In typographic terms it might be better to think of this concept as *consistency,* which can mean something as simple as always putting the page numbers in the same place on the pages, or using the same style and size for every heading of the same level.

But the implications of consistency reach further. The organizing principle behind layouts that depart from predictable columns and margins—ads, title pages, brochure covers and the like—is that every element in a layout such as this has a recognizable relationship with other elements on the page. Blocks of copy line up where they should; tag lines and illustrations create visual boundaries.

It should be possible for the reader to figure out a reason for the size, placement and style of each part and its role on the page. You can get away with all kinds of unusual design treatments if they're presented in a consistent fashion; remember the discussion about grouping your effects.

Involvement

One of the most visible failures of any design scheme, especially in the volatile world of printed words, is the obvious lack of commitment and care on the part of the producer/publisher. Perhaps the most dynamic quality you can instill in any page (or screen) layout is the sense that it was important enough to warrant an extra bit of time to resize a head or try a different typeface, and that you enjoyed producing it.

It's rare for any typographic structure to come out exactly right the first time, but these adjustments toward better appearance are among the subliminal appreciations the reader uses to decide whether a piece of visual language is worth pursuing.

If you feel these goals fail to embrace the nobler concepts of truth and beauty, keep in mind that the day's work strives for higher ideals, but it still must be the day's work. Rarely is a specimen of typography judged as a work of art; it's in the coherent and accurate assembly of the parts that a piece of desktop publishing achieves its true purpose: having the appropriate effect on the reader.

Creating Your Design and Layout

CHAPTER EIGHT

Creating Your Design and Layout

So, where does the design process start? First you need to ask yourself some questions: What am I trying to make? Who will read it? What should it look like? How do I get there?

By knowing what the thing is, you've gone a long way toward deciding what it should look like. And in the process you've begun to answer the question, How do I get there? You'll find you're making design decisions without being aware that you're doing so. The mental images you create in trying to answer these questions form the context for the real text and the first trial settings you pour into page margins.

For example, you may not notice that you *design* a business letter every time you set one up, since you do it several times a day and the procedure is second nature to you. Nevertheless, design decisions are involved. Whether you know it or not, if you deal with words on paper or screens, you're a designer.

What Is It?

What you're trying to make may seem self-evident. But if your business letter stretches out into a report, or your folded flyer becomes a brochure, the design will be different. Screens require an entirely different approach from print, and slides in color must be designed differently from pages made into overheads.

What you're going to make is dependent to some degree on how you can best reach a particular readership with a particular message. The decisions will involve the writers and editors, if any, as well as the originating sources of the project and the money required or available. For some projects, you might expect whole drifts of trial dummies, rough comps or rewritten text before the "design" emerges.

Who Will Read It?

If your answer is "everybody," then you must make a different thing than if you say "young rock 'n' roll fanatics." Do your readers include elderly folks with poor eyesight? (If so, avoid making a newsletter with unusual and difficult typography.) Or are they young and eager to experiment? From another perspective, if your audience is two dozen fellow employees, your tone, typographic style and production methods will be different than if you're writing to several thousand employees nationwide or publishing for general market sales.

Typography is so closely tied to the needs and expectations of the intended reader that it's foolish to begin designing, even choosing a text face, without answering this question. Type size, leading, format, writing and editorial decisions should all be made with regard to the readers you hope to address.

Even where the readership is "everybody," there's still a ghost reader that the written material is intended to reach. It may not be as obvious as a menu for the Octogenarian Society luncheon, but the ghost reader lurks in the writing, tone and style of every publication.

What Should It Look Like?

If you're producing a rock newsletter, how do you design it so it doesn't come out looking like a legal brief? And, perhaps more important, how can you make sure a legal brief doesn't come out looking like a rock newsletter?

We've seen that many of the distinctions can be made by the typefaces you choose, and we've looked at many of them, from several perspectives. Many types would work for both rock and legalese, so you're still left with the problem. If all you have is Times New Roman for your text, and you can say it will (or must) function in both environments, then what approach do you use to make the necessary distinctions clear?

The Legal Question

There's more involved here than merely wedding form and function. Although the size of the paper, the way it's folded, the number of columns and the density of the type can be revealing, the overall impression—the tone of a piece—comes together out of a gathering of visual images created by the secondary elements.

The size of the paper, the way it's folded, the number of columns and the density of the type can be revealing, the overall impression—the tone of a piece—comes together out of a gathering of visual images created by the secondary elements. There's more involved here than merely wedding form and function. Although the size of the paper, the way it's folded, the number of columns and the density of the type can be revealing, the overall impression—the tone of a piece—comes together out of a gathering of visual images created by the secondary elements. There's more involved here than merely wedding form and function.

Although the size of the paper, the way it's folded, the number of columns and the density of the type can be revealing, the overall impression—the tone of a piece—comes together out of a gathering of visual images created by the secondary elements. There's more involved here than merely wedding form and function. Although the size of the paper, the way it's folded, the number of columns and the density of the type can be revealing, the overall impression—the tonThere's more involved here than merely wedding form and function. Although the size of the paper, the way it's folded, the number of columns The size of the paper, the way it's folded, the number of columns and the density of the type can be revealing, the overall impression—the tone of a piece—comes together out of a gathering of visual images created by the secondary elements. There's more involved here than merely wedding form and function. Although the size of the paper, the way it's folded, the number of columns and the density of the type can be revealing, the overall impression—the tone of a piece—comes together out of a gathering of visual images created by the secondary elements. There's more involved here than merely wedding form and function.

Although the size of the paper, the way it's folded, the number of columns and the density of the type can be revealing, the overall impression—the tone of a piece—comes together out of a gathering of visual images created by the secondary elements. There's more involved here than merely wedding form and

December

Rock

The Music Rocks On

There's more involved here than merely wedding form and function. Although the size of the paper, the way it's folded, the number of columns and the density of the type can be revealing, the overall im-

Boneman Watson struts his stuff.

In This Issue

…Boneman

…History

…Together

…Forever

…The Music

…Concerts

Rock is published quarterly by the Rock International Group

pression—the tone of a piece—comes together out of a gathering of visual images created by the secondary elements. Although the size of the paper, the way it's folded, the number of columns and the density of the type can be revealing, the overall impression—the tone of a piece—comes together out of a gathering of visual images created by the secondary elements. Al-

ing, the overall impression—the tone of a piece—comes together out of a gathering of visual images created by the secondary elements. Although the size of the paper, the way it's folded. There's more involved here than merely wedding form and function. Although the size of the paper, the way it's folded, the number ofcolumns and the density of the type can be reveal-

There's more involved here than merely wedding form and function. Although the size of the paper, the way it's folded, the number of columns and the density of the type can be revealing, the overall impression—the tone of a piece—comes together out of a gathering of visual images created by the secondary elements.

How Big Should It Be?

My brother the carpenter claims he can build anything, as long as he knows how big you want it to be. In reading about a beast called the electric catfish in the encyclopedia one day, I learned that the only criterion for inclusion in the diet of that fish is size: "The electric catfish will eat anything, as long as it is the right size."

If you think about it, size is as important to the maker of typographic objects as it is to a builder or to an electric catfish. In fact, it may be the most important organizing feature of any construction. Once the question of size, or format, is settled, a number of other questions are automatically resolved. The early stages of any design project involve groping toward the appropriate size; and any time the size changes, you start over.

Size is often determined by production methods or other practical constraints. Laser printers accept certain paper sizes, as do photocopiers. And while printing presses are designed to print a variety of formats, they do have maximum and minimum limits. Material is also a factor. Paper is sold in standard sizes, so the designer's creative indulgence must be tempered by a concern for cost and wastage.

As another example, I'm working right now on a pamphlet that must fit inside a 6- by 9-inch envelope, the largest size possible that avoids a postal surcharge. Yet design and production considerations beg for a larger format. Mailing weights, two-sided printing, binding techniques and—to a certain extent—tradition can all be factors in determining a format.

First Steps

In typography, the design process starts with the writing—words first. The typographer is essentially putting into permanent visual form what the writer or editor envisioned.

When we speak, we rarely make an effort to design what we're saying. Words flow in the context of speech, and the design is subconscious. But in the act of writing, design begins. Where talking is spontaneous, writing is deliberate.

The author applies design principles by creating a pattern, a beginning, middle and end, arranging parts or elements in a certain order to create a whole thing—a text. The writer needs some design concept, some idea of the finished form of the work in order to proceed. Sometimes this form emerges after the writing has progressed. And sometimes design reaches only the level of deciding whether to go on to a second page or end the letter on the first.

As a typographer, you begin with an understanding of the text and the preliminary design decisions that are an integral part of the writing. The typography should present and elucidate the writing as effectively as possible.

Making It Happen: Conceptualization

Where do good ideas come from? How do you make them happen? How do you develop the knack of working from both ends, the manuscript in hand and the image of printed copies or finished screens in the mind's eye?

Creating typography can be broken into several stages: thumbnail sketches, dummy, trial proof, specifications and budget. They don't follow in any particular order, and each element varies in importance depending on the project. In conceptualizing, the primary tools are the thumbnail sketch and the dummy; they give concrete form to ideas and plans.

Thumbnail sketches might go through many revisions and end up with a very finished quality by the time a final layout is achieved.

A dummy is necessary for any folded piece or sequence of pages (or screens). For a book or a complex brochure, changing page counts and formats may generate a deskful of dummies.

It seems to me that the freshest ideas come at the thumbnail and dummy stages. At this point, there's no commitment: if the concept is no good, you can throw it away or save the good ideas for the next round of sketching.

The Thumbnail Sketch

This first rough draft of a project is usually done with a pencil, felt-tip pen, crayon or other instrument held in the hand. Although it's possible to run up preliminary thumbnails on your page layout program, it's hard to avoid a finished quality even in the early stages of work done on the screen. Computer-generated thumbnails are more useful for checking sequences and relationships across a large project. Soft pencil on newsprint is the traditional method at this early stage, to capture the nervous energy and fugitive fragments of inspiration, without being too precise, accurate or even correct.

You'll learn to see ideas emerge out of these rough drawings, and to lose whatever inhibitions you may have about doing them. It's such a useful method that I encourage everyone coming to typography not to be bashful, throw away those bad early attempts and begin learning to think with a pencil. You'll be surprised at how much your subsequent work will benefit from doing these preliminary sketches.

It's important for the sketch to be proportional in shape to the thing intended. If the shape is still an undeveloped part of the idea, try to establish the proportions as soon as possible. When size and shape are settled, then the sketch must follow that format; otherwise what you draw—type size, margins, etc.—will be misleading.

The Dummy

If you take a stack of scratch paper and start folding it, you can come up with some very interesting origami. If you take everything folded at right angles, you get pages that can be put together as printed pieces. If you number those leaves in various sequences (this is all without even a manuscript at hand), you begin to see the complexity possible in the way information is ordered and presented. One of the most interesting shapes, and a very common one, is the six-panel brochure made out of one sheet of standard paper folded in thirds. The variations on this theme are inexhaustible.

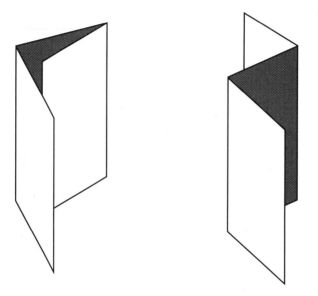

The dummy and the thumbnails go hand in hand; at certain stages in the thinking process, they're one and the same—as a sequence is applied to a fold pattern, for example.

Trial Proofs

After the thumbnails and the format decisions come the first settings. This once was a major commitment of time, where everything was set permanently in lead or on costly photographic paper. Now, on the computer screen we can see both roughs (in the small screen reproductions) and more finished settings—on full-page monitors or as parts enlarged to print size on the screen.

The ideal situation is to be able to move the type around, then evaluate the changes. In the old days, the typographer actually manipulated the type by hand before the printed evidence (the "proof") was produced. As the letters came together in little blocks, the printer could get an idea of how things were looking. Often, changes were made right at the assembly stage because a certain size or face didn't fit, or obviously wasn't going to look right, and further evidence wasn't needed.

In a way, we've returned to the precision of those days with the development of interactive forms in typography. Gone are the days when type was set according to codes known only to technicians of the esoteric. Gone are the days when type sizes were lead blocks that once cast could never change. And gone too are the limitations of a photographic image locked into a mechanical assembly device.

A new era in typography began when it became possible for the typographer to "try things out" so freely. The designer can now try out a score of possibilities for setting a given text and never have to pay the price of composition time or costly proofing.

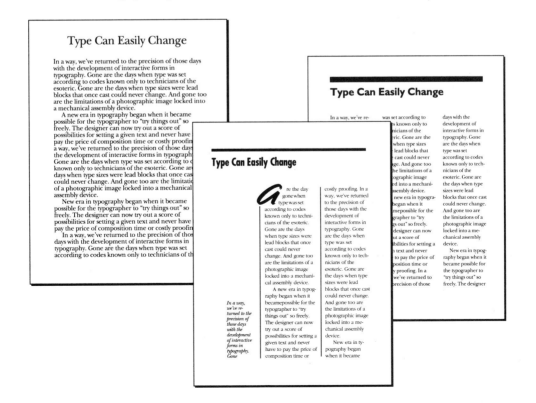

Remember that the proof is the key. From rough thumbnail to the final check before copies are printed, decisions are made along the way that bring the printed image ever closer to being the perfect vehicle for the things said. And these proofs don't necessarily have to be on paper.

Two Approaches to the Layout

There are many ways of allotting space to the complex of elements that make up newsletters and reports—headings, photographs, captions, sidebars and the like—so that each element is integrated with the overall piece. In most cases, a page design device commonly known as "the grid" is used. Grids can simplify the logical placement of a publication's many diverse parts.

Whole texts have been written by designers showing elaborate methods for dividing up pages into a visual network, sometimes containing scores of intricate divisions.

Grids

Any layout is consciously or subconsciously based on a grid, to maintain the orderliness of reading and avoid confusion. This invisible structure assures that the parts of a piece are logically connected and that disparate elements aren't hooked together.

Expressed another way, any planned relationship of parts on a page can be viewed as a grid, even if it's only a single column of type with margins stretching to the edge of the page. If the margins and type column are sized in proportion to the page, then elements are divisible into units, some of them occupied by type, some by white space.

If you add other typographic elements—a page number, footnote, subhead and so on—you have a more complex grid. This fundamental geometric and architectural approach to printed pages helps maintain the consistency so necessary for effective publications.

But as the page layout is divided into ever smaller units to accommodate a mass of diverse parts, the grid can become self-defeating, as its inner logic is lost in a maze of subtle relationships. For example, you may have a large number of photographs of radically differing shapes and sizes, with captions of varying lengths, plus a hierarchy of subsidiary headings and a sidebar.

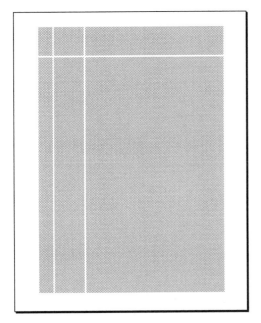 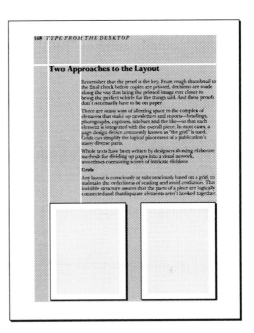

Strict reliance on an intricate grid is especially dangerous when a ragged-right setting is used for all or part of the text, and where the disposition of white space determines much of the visual impact.

Organic Layout

There's another way of looking at page layout that allows the conditions of the setting to determine the layout structure. It's called an "organic" design approach, because it treats the page (or the spread) as a "field," in which, within the constraints of a few established parameters such as consistent margins, the typography finds its own natural balance of sizes, shapes and white space.

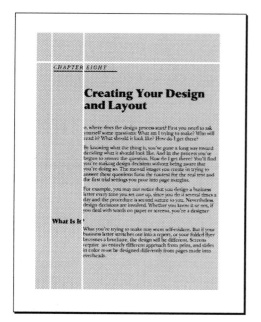

Grid   Organic

The "organic" approach relies a great deal on visual balance (squinting), while the grid relies heavily on structure.

In the early days of page design, to break the constraints of leaden rectangles (or photographic assemblers, for that matter) was an arduous task; to stretch into a margin just because it looked better was often so hard to do that it wasn't practical. (Remember that in the old days white space was also created with solid objects.)

If you choose to set ragged text, with its uneven margins, you create a complex of irregular shapes that would make a grid structure hard to define—especially a complicated one. In a really good grid-based design, notice that seemingly asymmetrical elements are actually part of the overall scheme.

Within the general confines of the outside margins and a consistent beginning reference point for each page, the elements of an organic asymmetrical structure may have to be arranged in peculiar ways, to make use of the vibrant relationship of white spaces. Parts may leap out into the margins, stuck there because of the oddities of visual centering or balance.

This same defiance of limits is used to good effect in grid layouts, too, but a grid doesn't quite work if the logic of it is too well hidden.

Adhering strictly to grid.

Breaking out of the grid.

Letting Form Follow Function

You set up parameters when you choose your margin settings at the outset of your work. But as soon as you place any piece of type, especially in a display size, the shapes of that type redefine the margins you have set arbitrarily. If you then proceed by relying on the logic of those black and white text shapes, keeping visual balance and tension as your goal, then your pages will present the text at hand better than any grid or preset margins could.

In my work, I like to set all margins at zero and treat the page as an open field. Later I can come back and set a series of guides to act as anchors for margins and placements that must be consistent from page to page. This approach sometimes means working with a lot of different flagged pieces, and it can be confusing if you're not careful. The point is that this approach allows you to bring the parts of a layout together based on how they really look, rather than make type choices that force them to fit.

The elements of the design process are intricate and involve many decisions, all made interdependently. I have attempted to give you a method for putting an often chaotic picture into some kind of order. Your job is to keep reworking the parts until they all fit together.

CHAPTER NINE

Production

Production

For all its remarkable capabilities, a desktop publishing system is a minor, though important, player in the printing and publishing industry. The digital layout is often only one in a series of skilled operations involving sophisticated tools and lots of time and money. I'm still amazed at how far these personal systems can go with complex visual technologies. But if we're to do our best work, we must accept our limitations. Our skills as typographic designers do not make us capable of doing color checks on a six-unit web press.

However, it is part of a typographer's job to be familiar with the processes and facilities that may be needed for final production, such as high-resolution image setters, offset duplicators, slide-generating equipment and color webs. It's especially important to know when to retain the services of experts and specialists. More about this later.

Know Your Tools

Let's be honest and admit right here that type does not look its best reproduced at 300 dots to the inch. On the other hand, you should know that type doesn't necessarily look its best reproduced by photographic processes at resolutions of 1,270 to 2,540 dpi (dots per inch). The image type presents is made when the ink meets the paper; the quality of that image is directly connected with the methods by which this meeting happens.

Because of the difficulty in predicting the quality of the final image, you must pay close attention to the systems you have in place. Despite advances being made in establishing standards for page description, type quality and printer resolution, your assembly of hardware and software is still a contributing factor to the quality of the output.

The number of possible combinations of personal computer, page layout software, printer configuration and typeface supplier stagger the imagination. So there's no easy way to know how to address problems in getting the kind of images you want—except to say that the entire system has to be compatible.

Much depends on the kind of work you produce. If you do in-house newsletters and correspondence, you may never work to an image setter. Therefore your desktop printer must be more than a proofing device, capable of the best resolution quality possible. On the other hand, a medium-resolution desktop printer would be a waste of money for a designer using it merely to proof layouts on their way to photographic paper or film.

If you're determined (for whatever reason) to use nothing but resident fonts, your equipment can be cheaper and less conventional than what you'd need if you wanted to use downloadable fonts and imported graphics. Industry standards are changing and evolving. Therefore, the broader your graphic resource base, the closer you should keep to standards that don't obstruct your access to tools and images. Don't buy junk.

Since you can't tell how different printers will interact with different imaging technologies on different papers, all you can do is develop a keen eye for the standard of quality you're trying to achieve.

Our view of the way printed letters ought to look has changed over time. When they were printed from raised metal images onto hand-made stock, letters had the same roughness as the methods used to make and print them. But with the refinement of letterform design and drawing, finer materials were required. Baskerville produced innovations in both paper and ink to better display the fine lines of the type he had developed.

Coated stock and photographic technology have changed our expectations for realizing letter refinements to the point where the thins in types like Baskerville or Bodoni nearly disappear. There's a contradiction in making type to reproduce at vastly differing degrees of refinement. Some digital typefaces have different versions for different resolutions—Optima and Prospera are examples.

Coated stock and photographic technology have changed our expectations for realizing letter refinements to the point where the thins in types like Baskerville or Bodoni nearly disappear. There's a contradiction in making type to reproduce at vastly differing degrees of refinement. Some digital typefaces have versions for different resolutions—Optima and Prospera

Optima at medium resolution.

Coated stock and photographic technology have changed our expectations for realizing letter refinements to the point where the thins in types like Baskerville or Bodoni nearly disappear. There's a contradiction in making type to reproduce at vastly differing degrees of refinement. Some digital typefaces have versions for different resolutions—Optima and Prospera

Optima at high resolution.

For many, laser printer resolutions are adequate, so perhaps our expectations are beginning to swing back the other way—away from the sharp, perfectly clean lines of photography to the coarser, bulkier feel of antique printing. Somewhere in between lies an acceptable standard that achieves adequate clarity of form and line on "plain" paper without relying on over-refined, costly and chemically harmful photographic processes.

As I write, plain-paper copiers capable of resolutions up to 1,000 dots to the inch are becoming available and in some cases cost-effective. Meanwhile, discovering tricks for getting the best out of whatever printing device you have can improve image quality considerably. Machine adjustments, different papers or other typeface choices can change the look of the output. For offset printing and photocopying, images can be printed out oversized, then reduced, effectively increasing the resolution.

Service Bureaus

In situations where your pages will be going to offset presses—where there are halftone photographs, colors, screens or where it makes sense to set directly to film—high-resolution photographic images may be essential. Most desktop publishers use professional typesetting services for this work. In addition to providing access to expensive equipment and specialized skills, these "service bureaus" maintain very extensive type libraries. They're a good resource for faces you want to use only occasionally.

Consult with service bureaus available to you about compatibility of hardware and software, and about procedures for getting the best out of the equipment. If you use your laser printer as a proofing device, you can go directly to film in most cases, saving the cost and material of printing on photographic paper. But output pages are costly on these image setters, so you should learn ways to group pages together to take advantage of film or paper sizes and standard procedures to avoid costly mistakes.

I must say that fine work is being done at all resolutions on all sorts of printers, from Quickdraw midgets on up—offset, quick-print, photocopy and direct. Good work is not dependent on technology.

Talking to Real Printers

Because your computer-designed pages may require color, unusual sizes and folds, large quantities or numbers of pages, your work will quickly lead you to professional printing. Printing companies come in various sizes and types, and services range from duplicating to major publication production. One problem is choosing the right one, so that you don't expect a highly technical piece of work from a quick-print shop, or pay the price of full-size press work for a job that could be done on a small duplicator.

Booklet, 4¼"x7"

Flyer, 8½"x3½"

Brochure
8½"x8½" with
2½" return stub

Begin by learning about presses located nearby, but keep in mind that in some cases, especially publication printing, you may end up sending your work halfway across the country to obtain a certain kind of production. Normally, it's far easier to work directly with the printing facility, especially if you're inexperienced. You can learn a lot from talking to people at print shops.

It's important that you engage printing services early enough in your own planning process to allow for delays or other unexpected complications. The printer will also want to know about quantity, size, type of paper, bindery needs and the like. The sales teams of most printing facilities are experienced in providing working plans for the projects they handle. The sooner you can provide these details, the quicker the costs can be figured and the more accurate they'll be. Thumbnail sketches, dummies and clear alternatives for quantities and materials make the estimating, scheduling and assembling phases of a job easier for the printer.

After you've offered your requirements, then sit back and listen. There are tricks and techniques for doing things to pieces of paper that may astound you. If you let a printing planner suggest possibilities—foil stamping, die cutting, unusual bindings, interesting folds, ways of using color effectively, clever combinations of colored ink and colored papers—you may come up with an approach to your project you'd never have discovered otherwise.

And the more time you give to the planning, the better the results. If you set up a workable schedule, and stick to your end of it, you won't be forcing the printing facility to do hasty work to meet an unreasonable deadline—although the fact is that printers are frequently under intolerable deadline pressures.

By advance planning, listening to ideas and possibilities and setting reasonable schedules, you can establish good working relationships with printing companies, and thereby improve the quality and originality of your work as you learn and develop your skills.

Other Expert Help

Because graphic arts comprise many specialties, you should be prepared to seek out experts in other areas besides printing production. Photographers, illustrators, writers, editors and occasionally specialty design experts may be called in to help on projects that go beyond your facilities or capabilities. For the intricate typography of an instruction manual or an annual report, you should feel it's okay to bring in design skills you don't possess. Professionals who know about color, the subtleties of reproducing halftones, or how to integrate technical drawings and text can move things right along, whereas your own trial and error might take too long and send you off the rails. Most areas have graphic arts associations that can supply the names of competent specialists.

Selecting Paper

If you're new to this game of typography, you probably haven't spent much time staring at blank sheets of paper—unless you're afflicted with the writer's disease. But you'll begin to do so as your ideas on the screen become real objects in print.

The relationship of paper to the work you do is fundamental; the nature, quality and colors of the paper you choose can exert a powerful influence. Paper is a significant cost factor in print production, and the way you apply your budget to your material will make a difference in the appearance of your publication.

Paper is magical stuff, despite the fact we take it for granted. The manufacture of paper is an awesome process. Huge machines grind up wood pulp and other ingredients and spew out the end product on monstrous rolls. There's something intriguing and mysterious about a substance that seems so fragile yet is so tough that it might last hundreds of years.

Paper and type have been inextricably connected since printing was invented. We can still learn from and adapt the typographic genius of the past by going to libraries and looking at Gutenberg Bibles,

Ring

Staple

Glue

Aldine pocket editions and original Garamond types—all printed on ancient paper.

The past 20 years have seen a renewed interest in making paper by hand and in increasing the durability of machine-made paper. Workshops are given frequently around the country by experts in hand-papermaking techniques. You can experience the magic of forming a sheet of the stuff by attending one of these classes.

Just becoming familiar with commercial papers can also help you as a designer a great deal. The paper typically found by the ream and by the case in businesses, around copying machines and in print shops is called "bond." Bond papers have gone through interesting transformations in recent years as paper-makers try to come up with content formulations that work best for laser printing. Plain white bond has been made smoother and somewhat more opaque.

Excellent results can be achieved with the right combination of paper and printer. You'll need to experiment with various grades and finishes to find the paper that works best with your tools. Bond papers are available for laser printers in standard business sizes. And like it or not, these are what you'll use for most of the work you do, even if they aren't very interesting. They're usually available in a range of colors, however. High-quality bond papers, with rag content and good subtle colors and textures, are also available for all kinds of business printing.

If you want interesting paper, you can use a grade called "text." These papers have the colors, textures and weights suitable for commercial work such as print advertising, brochures, annual reports and the like, and the range is extensive. Costs for these papers are considerably higher than for standard bonds, and you may find that the coarse textures and heavier weights will not function in your desktop printer. Either the paper won't feed because it's too heavy, or the xerographic image won't transfer properly to the textured surface. On the other hand, type, even from a laser printer, looks best on a slightly textured paper.

Some printers handle heavier weights than others; ink-jet printers may not have the transfer problem of those based on xerography. You should test the limits of your desktop printer so you'll know the extent of its capabilities as a part of the design process.

For any project that demands unusual papers, you should get in touch with your printing company to discuss the wide variety of papers available, the pros and cons of using offset printing, and whether you'll need bindery services for your publication.

Type of Papers	Description	Uses
Copier/Laser	smooth, generally inexpensive	copy machines, laser printers
Uncoated Offset	smooth, dull finish	general-purpose printing and duplication
Coated Offset	very smooth, gloss or dull finish	quality printing , best for multi-color & photos
Writing/Bond	toothy, soft paper, high fiber content	stationery, invitations, business cards
Text & Cover	colors, textures, finishes, uncoated	brochures, folders, flyers, promotional materials
Specialty	adhesive-backed papers, boards	labels, stickers, signs

In planning publications it's very useful to know the standard sizes of papers and printing presses. It's easy to obtain this information from paper wholesalers and commercial printers.

As you become more knowledgeable, you can play the game I call "printer's origami," in which the designer attempts to fold, cut and trim standard paper sizes into unusual money-saving and workable new shapes.

But keep in mind that paper has an intrinsic directional "grain," formed during its manufacture, that strongly influences the way the publication must be folded or bound. Grain direction is given in all paper specimen books.

Paper Conservation & Recycling

It's hard to get used to the idea that paper is a precious commodity. It comes to us in reams, bundles and heaps—in consumer packaging, business correspondence, junk mail and fat Sunday newspapers. The flow seems continuous and inexhaustible. In fact, we spend a lot of time and effort getting rid of it.

In our gluttonous consumption of paper, we've put a lot of pressure on a fragile resource that we should be nurturing as part of our global life-support system. Conifer forests exert an important stabilizing influence on the water and the air.

Wood fibers make lousy paper, compared to many other accessible fibers. They're short and not as strong as cotton, linen, sisal or hemp, for example. And what's worse, an environmentally intrusive process is required to release those fibers from their woody composition and bleach them white. We use wood fiber for the manufacture of paper because it's plentiful and cheap, and because it fits a certain industrial model firmly established in our economic pattern.

One promising aspect of the digital revolution in the graphic arts is the prospect of a reduction in the "paper stream." It's already happening. Electronic mail is reducing the mountains of paper in the business environment. Electronic manuscripts have replaced much of the paper used in the past by literary wretches like us. Even the fax machine, the ubiquitous new business toy, reduces the need for material, despite its high costs in other areas.

Recycling paper products has gone in and out of fashion, and it's still often difficult to find suitable recycled materials for certain projects, such as books. Recycling can have a high environmental cost in terms of the dioxins used to return the paper to a pristine whiteness. But made properly, recycled paper represents a tremendous saving of both energy and resources.

Recycling is a state of mind and we need to make it a way of life. By recycling our paper—all kinds—and using recycled stock whenever possible, we become aware of how much of these resources we use and can move toward a balance of consumption and conservation.

I'm writing in an era in which the way we look at and produce printed material is changing rapidly. By the time you read this, we may be designing typographic pages that never leave the electronic medium. Already the planning of typographic screen presentations is a major part of many designers' work. As television and the computer find a common digital medium, it will be possible for much wasteful production of print to be eliminated.

I think that as you become more involved in typography, you'll come to appreciate paper for the unusually valuable substance it is. I hope you'll join me in trying to find ways to treat it with due respect. This could mean figuring out a way to eliminate that trial sheet laser printers always run at start-up; encouraging two-sided printing in our offices; or supporting the good recycled sheets available through local printshops. We don't have to give paper up; we just have to learn to respect it.

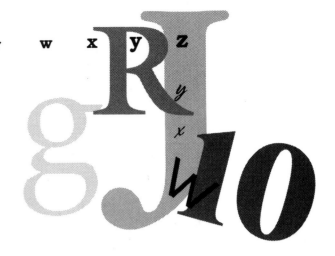

Money, Time & Fun

Money, Time & Fun

Expressing language visually has always been subject to constraints: the limits of technology, access to materials and processes, merciless deadlines and tender budgets. But that's where the fun begins.

In publishing—as in any other endeavor—overcoming these obstacles—meeting the challenge and accomplishing something you can look at with pride—is satisfying to the soul.

Money

Money has a powerful and usually limiting influence in all aspects of disseminating information and ideas in printed form. First, there's never *enough* money. But by making do with the budget you have and reaching down deep into your creative wellspring, you can make something interesting and demonstrate that money isn't everything in the presentation of an idea.

Second, expensive, extravagant typography is often entirely out of place. Verbal presentations must be appropriate to the value of the work involved. Ephemera, throw-aways, shouldn't have the same budget lavished on them as works that are meant to last. Conversely, you can destroy the effect of an important piece—an annual report, for example—through sloppy assembly or crummy materials, making it look like it was done on the cheap.

In these days of very accessible typefaces by the thousands, don't forget that some of the greatest printing has been done with only one typeface in one size. For example, take a look at the work of the renowned Doves Press, whose stunning books were all printed from a single font.

It's easy to be seduced by the new tools, the new typefaces, and thereby lose the creative advantage inherent in the limitation of resources. What is the advantage of a hard disk full of typefaces if all those faces do is clutter your pages?

And, speaking of new tools, another delightful toy that can be abused is the color monitor and the programs for generating color printing. For some work it can be an essential tool, but for pure typography, where crisp black on white is the ideal, it can be a hindrance.

Another mitigating factor in severely limited production budgets—one that may actually improve your projects—is that you can maintain control of creative solutions, rather than relying on a lot of color, whiz-bang paper or expensive graphic effects.

Always an acceptable and effective device to create variety, careful and restrained manipulation of typefaces is a good substitute where graphic pyrotechnics are unaffordable.

New ways of presenting language in its simplest form—black ink on white paper—are anything but exhausted. There's always "new typography" that costs nothing but creative imagination. New faces, new ways of using the old ones, and combinations no one has thought of are just waiting to be discovered.

Time

Limited time, on the other hand, can be a bigger problem. In the planning and execution of typographic design, too little time spent means overlooking many small refinements that can make the difference between dull, ordinary pages and those that sing with insight and precision.

I've said this before, but it bears repeating: it's a fallacy that the digital medium eliminates the hazards of making last-minute changes. In this case, the medium cannot replace the human factor. It takes time and a critical eye to look at proofs and work out adjustments needed to make a piece of typography click into place visually. It takes whatever time it takes, just as it takes time to learn the characteristics and effects of various typefaces and how to use them in different circumstances.

None of this changes the reality of deadlines or the fact that any publication must be timely or lose its chance. But it may convince you to allow time to step back from the rush of production and identify those final adjustments of alignment, spacing and fitting that can contribute significantly to a successful piece of work.

If you have your choice between time and money, take the time.

Fun

I've spoken about the reawakening of my love affair with Caslon in its digital form—the thrill of seeing it hold up on a piece of handmade paper hand-fed through a Laserwriter Plus. And I could go on about the pleasure of finding out that another typographic inamorata, the Perpetua typeface, looks pretty good in the new medium; the ease of kerning with buttons instead of a file and saw; and the kick I get from setting Stone Serif at 127 points, just because it was never possible before.

Perhaps I'm too easily impressed, but when the Adobe Type Manager came along and allowed me for the first time to see the innards of typefaces right there on the screen, I felt recharged with enthusiasm for playing with letters for their own sake. I found myself once again happily peeking inside the alphabet for new discoveries of shape and space.

As you delve deeper into typography, you'll be able to recount your own special experiences and discoveries. Try to remember always that your work should give you pleasure, although you can't expect to revel in the sheer joy of it when the pressure's on. But typography, whether you pursue it for employment or as a hobby, is a craft that offers infinite variety, the richness of our language, old and new, and the skills of some of the world's great artists.

Okay, have fun.

Glossary

Ascender: (See also Descender; x-height.) The part of a letter such as b, d, f, h, k, l that sticks up above the "x-height." An ascender must be tall enough to be recognized as such quickly; if the ascender is out of proportion to the x-height, legibility suffers.

Bit-mapped: Made up of individual dots.

Blackletter: Typeface style based on regional handwriting current at the time printing was invented.

Boldface: A heavy, or darker, weight of a typeface, often used for emphasis.

Bowl: The space inside the circular part(s) of a letter (e.g., p and o).

Broadside: A large sheet of paper printed on one side (e.g., with a political message).

Centered alignment: An alignment scheme in which lines of type are centered over each other or over a body of text.

Counter: (See also Bowl.) Space inside a letter that opens onto the white space between words (e.g., c and s).

Descender: (See also Ascender; x-height.) Parts of letters such as g, j, p, q and y that fall below the baseline, or reading line, of type. If they're too truncated (often done to increase the x-height) the grace and balance of the typeface may suffer.

Digitizing: The technology that uses patterns of tiny dots to create letters and other typeface characters.

Dingbats: Small decorative marks used in printing, such as "bullets," boxes and other small graphics. Usually available as a set on a separate font.

Display type: Usually a larger or heavier version or contrasting typeface to differentiate headings from text.

DPI: Dots per inch.

Drop cap: An initial letter, the top of which aligns horizontally with the tops of ascenders and uppercase letters in the first line of type.

Drop shadow: A graphic effect that places a shadow behind an image, such as a boxed table or list. The shadow is offset slightly below and to one side.

Dummy: Folded pages with roughed-in layout features, created as a preliminary mock-up for a publication.

Ellipsis: A three-dot punctuation figure indicating omitted words.

Flush-left alignment: An alignment scheme in which type is aligned with the left margin, creating an uneven right margin.

Flush-right alignment: An alignment scheme in which type is aligned with the right margin, leaving an uneven left margin.

Folio: In published work, a page number; also in periodicals a term used for publication date and issue information.

Font: One member of a typeface family, such as bold, italic or bold italic. All uppercase and lowercase letters, figures, punctuation and special characters of a font are accessible from the keyboard.

Grid: An underlying pattern of lines used by the designer to divide a page into layout spaces.

Gutter: Margins between two facing pages; also vertical space separating type columns.

Halftone photo: A photograph rendered into a pattern of dots or lines for the printing process.

Hyphenation: See Justification and hyphenation.

Initial letters (or initial caps): Display-size letters used as decoration or graphic devices.

Italic: A slanted design version of a typeface, usually based on handwriting, used as a companion to roman type.

Justification and hyphenation: An alignment scheme for setting text that uses hyphenation and word spacing to make all lines the same length in a column or on a page. Justified lines produce even rather than uneven margins.

Kerning: (See also Tracking.) The fitting together of certain pairs of letters to take up unnecessary space between them for enhanced appearance and legibility.

Layout: The arrangement of type and graphic elements on a page or screen.

Leading (or line spacing): White space between lines of type. The proper amount of leading is a key factor in readability.

Letter spacing: (See also Kerning.) Adjusting (sometimes adding) space between letters. While some letter combinations need to be tucked up, others need to be slightly separated to look good.

Ligature: Two letters written or printed as one character (e.g.,fi, fl, æ).

Margin: (See also White space.) The white space around a column of type. Margins set off type in the same way that a mat or a frame sets off a picture.

Modern: Type design that moved away from the shapes of letters made with a pen to purely invented letter shapes. Modern types have strong contrast, abrupt transition between thick and thin strokes, and vertically and horizontally oriented accents.

Old Style: Type designs developed during the late 15th century through the middle of the 18th century, including Bembo (Italy, 1495); Garamond (France, 1530-60); Janson and Caslon.

Organic layout: A layout scheme that relies on visual balance rather than a grid structure.

Output: The final image on paper, film or screen; the only way to see what a typeface or other typographic element will look like after it's produced.

Pica: (See also Point.) The typographer's unit of measure. There are 12 points to a pica and six picas to the inch. This measuring system survived the digital revolution, probably because divisions in multiples of 12 are so easy to relate to. Line length specifications are usually given in picas.

Point: (See also Pica.) A subdivision of a pica and the traditional unit of typographic measure in most countries, equaling 1/72 of an inch. This happens to be the size of a pixel, or picture element, on most computer screens.

Printer: When printers became output devices rather than people who did printing, a certain amount of confusion arose that has not been completely worked out.

Pull-quotes: Excerpted phrases or sentences isolated from text, and set off in quotes or other display type treatment.

Resident font: A typeface built into a printer.

Resolution: The sharpness and clarity of an image produced on a screen or output to paper or film.

Reversed image: White type on a black or screened gray background.

Roman type: Upright, not slanted, type; often serif as opposed to sans-serif type.

Rules: Lines of various thickness, often decorative, used to form boxes, borders and other graphic separators.

Sans-serif: (See also Serif.) Types designed without finishing strokes, or serifs. They have straight stems and nearly monotone lines.

Script: Typeface design based on ornate steel-pen handwriting.

Serif: In typeface design, a "finishing stroke" such as a fillip or terminal crossbar, ranging in size from stubby triangles to razor-thin horizontal flicks.

Set-width: (See Tracking; Kerning.) The amount of space required to set a given line of text in a given typeface. Set-width is a function of x-height size, lateral compression of curves and generosity of serifs. In many programs, tracking adjustment makes a given typeface set tighter or looser.

Sidebar: A short article that relates to a longer piece of text, appearing on the same page, often boxed or set on a screened background.

Small caps: Uppercase letters traditionally set to the x-height of the text size.

Stem: In typeface design, an upright stroke in a letter or character.

Stress: Variation between thick and thin strokes of a type character.

Terminals: Ends of certain letter shapes that are not exactly serifs (e.g., a, f, j, r, y).

Thumbnail sketch: A simple, rough rendition, with pencil and paper or on screen, that helps to visualize how a design idea would look in a layout.

Tint: A shade of gray used under text or graphics.

Tracking: (See also Kerning.) A typesetting program adjustment that allows the typographer to alter the normal spacing of letters, to make them fit together tighter or looser.

Transitional: The term applied to typeface designs created in the late 18th century. Serifs were lightened, vertical stress was strengthened and general fineness of detail led to the Modern types of the next century.

Type family: A related collection of type fonts in various weights and versions, designed to work together. Famous type families include Univers and Cheltenham.

Type size: Once constrained by the capabilities of metal casting and photographic masters; now almost unlimited, thanks to universal outline codes rather than specific images.

Typeface: A design interpretation—often named after the designer—of a character set including letters, numbers and symbols.

Typography: The art and craft of choosing and assembling type elements to present the words at hand.

Uncial: A large, rounded, ancient letterform used in Greek and Latin script; a precursor of the lowercase alphabet.

x-height: (See also Ascender; Descender) The body size, excluding ascender and descender, of a letter (i.e., the height of a lowercase x) in any given typeface. X-height affects leading, readability and space requirements.

Bibliography

Adobe Systems Staff. *PostScript Language Tutorial & Cookbook.* Reading, MA: Addison-Wesley, 1985.

Anderson, Donald M. *The Art of Written Forms.* New York: Holt, Rinehart and Winston, 1969.

Arnheim, Rudolf. *Visual Thinking.* Berkeley, CA: University of California Press, 1980.

Barker, Nicolas. *Stanley Morison.* Cambridge, MA: Harvard University Press, 1972.

Bauermeister, Benjamin. *A Manual of Comparative Typography: The PANOSE System.* New York: Van Nostrand Reinhold, 1987.

Beaumont, Michael. *Type: Design, Color, Character & Use.* Cincinnati, OH: North Light Books, 1986.

Bennett, Paul, ed. *Books and Printing, A Treasury for Typophiles.* Cleveland, OH: World Publications, 1963.

Blumenthal, Joseph. *Art of the Printed Book, 1455-1955.* Boston, MA: David R. Godine, 1973.

Blumenthal, Joseph. *The Printed Book in America.* Hanover, NH: University Press of New England, 1989.

Burke, Clifford. *Printing It.* Berkeley, CA: Wingbow Press, 1974.

Burke, Clifford. *Printing Poetry.* San Francisco, CA: Scarab Press, 1980.

Carter, Rob, Day, Ben, and Meggs, Philip. *Typographic Design: Form and Communication.* New York: Van Nostrand Reinhold, 1985.

Chappell, Warren. *A Short History of the Printed Word.* Boston, MA: David R. Godine, 1980.

Editorial Staff of the University of Chicago Press. *The Chicago Manual of Style,* 13th ed. Chicago, IL: University of Chicago Press, 1982.

Craig, James. *Designing with Type: A Basic Course in Typography.* New York: Watson-Guptill, 1980.

Dair, Carl. *Design with Type.* Toronto: University of Toronto Press, 1982.

Durer, Albrecht. *Of the Just Shaping of Letters: From the Applied Geometry of Albrecht Durer, Book Three.* 1917. Reprint. New York: Dover Publications, 1965.

Fine Print Magazine. *Fine Print on Type: The Best of Fine Print Magazine on Type and Typography, 1977-1988.* San Francisco, CA: Bedford Arts, 1988.

Gill, Eric. *Eric Gill: An Essay on Typography.* Boston, MA: David R. Godine, 1989.

Goines, David Lance. *A Constructed Roman Alphabet.* Boston, MA: David R. Godine, 1982.

Goudy, Frederic W. *Goudy's Type Designs: His Story and Specimens.* New Rochelle, New York: Myriade Press, 1978.

Goudy, Frederic W. *The Alphabet and Elements of Lettering.* 1922. Reprint. New York: Dover, 1963.

Goudy, Frederic W. *Typologia: Studies in Type Design and Type Making.* 1940. Reprint. Berkeley, CA and Los Angeles, CA: University of California Press, 1978.

Hunter, Dard. *Papermaking.* 1947. Reprint. New York: Dover, 1978.

Hurlburt, Allen. *The Grid.* New York: Van Nostrand Reinhold, 1982.

Johnston, Edward. *Writing & Illuminating & Lettering.* 1906. Reprint. New York: Taplinger, 1977.

Kelly, Rob R. *American Wood Type: 1828-1900.* New York: Da Capo Press, 1977.

Lawson, Alexander. *Printing Types: An Introduction.* Boston, MA: Beacon Press, 1974.

Meggs, Philip B. *A History of Graphic Design.* New York: Van Nostrand Reinhold, 1983.

Morison, Stanley. *Letter Forms.* New York: The Typophiles, 1968.

Morison, Stanley. *A Tally of Types With Additions by Several Hands.* 1953. Revised. New Castle, DE: Oak Knoll Books, 1973.

Morison, Stanley, and Day, Kenneth. *The Typographic Book, 1450-1935.* Chicago, IL: The University of Chicago Press, 1964.

Neufeldt, Victoria, ed. *Webster's New World Dictionary, Third College Edition.* New York: Webster's New World, 1988.

Rogers, Bruce. *Paragraphs on Printing.* New York: Dover, 1980.

Romano, Frank J. *The TypEncyclopedia: A User's Guide to Better Typography.* New York: R.R. Bowker, 1984.

Updike, Daniel Berkeley. *Printing Types, Their History, Forms & Use.* 2d ed. 2 vols. 1962. Reprint. New York: Dover Publications, 1980.

White, Jan. *Graphic Design for the Electronic Age.* New York: Watson-Guptill, 1988.

Wilson, Adrian. *The Design of Books.* Salt Lake City, UT: Peregrine Smith, 1974.

Zapf, Hermann. *Hermann Zapf and His Design Philosophy.* New Haven, CT: Yale University Press, 1989.

Type Makers

Adobe Systems
1585 Charleston Road
P.O. Box 7900
Mountain View, CA 94039-7900
800-83-FONTS

Bitstream, Inc.
Athenaeum House
215 First Street
Cambridge, MA 02142
800-243-8088

Garrett Boge
LETTER-PERFECT
6606 Soundview Drive
Gig Harbor, WA 98335
206-851-5158

Casady & Greene, Inc.
P.O. Box 223779
Carmel, CA 93922
408-646-4660

The Font Company/URW
12629 N. Tatum Boulevard,
Suite 210
Phoenix, AZ 85032
602-996-2510

Peter Fraterdeus
Alphabets, Inc.
P.O. Box 5448
Evanston, IL 60204
800-326-4083

Giampa Textware
1340 E. Pender Street
Vancouver, B.C. V5L 1V8
604-253-0815

Kingsley ATF Type Corp.
2559-2 East Broadway
Tucson, AZ 85716
602-325-5884

The Linotype Co.
Type Sales
425 Oser Avenue
Hauppauge, NY 11788
800-633-1900

Monotype Typography, Inc.
53 W. Jackson Boulevard, Suite 504
Chicago, IL 60604
800-MONOTYPE

Judith Sutcliffe
The Electric Typographer
2216 Cliff Drive
Santa Barbara, CA 93109
805-966-7563

Typefaces Mentioned

American Uncial (Electric)   129

Avant Garde   107, 142

Baskerville   52, 58, 77, 105, 106, 107, 120, 121, 122, 126, 180, 181

Bembo   51, 52, 110, 126, 150

Berkeley Old Style   132

Blackletter types (Fluent laser Gregorian)   48, 128, 132

Blado   126

Bodoni   53, 58, 77, 106, 122, 151, 181

Bookman   104, 105

Broadway   131

Caledonia   106

Caslon   51, 52, 77, 104, 105, 106, 118, 126, 193

Century   105

Century Schoolbook   46, 60, 104, 105, 107

Cheltenham   75

Clarendon   54, 124

Dutch Old Face   106, 114

Futura   5, 107, 144

Galliard   55, 106, 116

Garamond   48, 51, 65, 104, 105, 106, 107, 112, 116, 120, 121, 122, 140, 151

Garamont   132

Gill Sans   48, 56, 142, 143

Glypha   125

Goudy New Style   132, 133

Goudy Modern   132

Goudy Old Style   55, 132

Granjon (Aldine 424)   116, 117

Hadriano   132

Helvetica   47, 56, 77, 80, 108, 118, 136, 137, 142, 146

International See Zapf.

Italia   131

Italian Old Style (Electric Italian)   106

Janson   51, 52, 65, 77, 105, 106, 114, 116, 126

Jenson   131

Kennerly   132

Libra   129

Lombardic Initials   132

Melior   54, 106

Memphis   54, 151

Michelangelo Titling   105

New Baskerville   52

New Century Schoolbook   46

Old Dreadful No. 7   45

Optima   56, 105, 140, 144, 146, 150, 181

Palatino   57, 60, 104, 105, 118, 138, 139, 146, 150, 151

Perpetua   193

Plantin   134

Poliphilus   126

Poster types   131

Prospera   181

Regency Script   130

Ritz Laser   131

Sabon   55, 106

Script types   130

Slimbach's Garamond   105, 106

Stone   65, 75, 76, 105, 107, 140, 150

Stone Sans   76

Stone Serif   5, 57, 76, 141, 193

Times Roman   47, 55, 59, 60, 77, 80, 105, 107, 114, 118, 122, 134, 135, 140

Times New Roman   134, 165

Uncial types   129

Univers   75

Utopian   54

Van Dijck   116, 117, 126

Zapf's types   93, 105, 106

Type Specifications for This Book

Body text

11-point New Baskerville Italic (Adobe); 14-point leading (11/14)
Column width: 27 picas
Paragraphs: block style (no indent)
Plus 7 points of lead between paragraphs

Headings

First Level	16/20 Perpetua Bold
	Flush-left on illustration margin
Second Level	14/16 Perpetua Bold
	Flush-left on text margin
Third Level	12/16 New Baskerville Bold Italic
	Flush-left on text margin

Chapter opening pages

Chapter No.	14-point New Baskerville Italic
	Flush-left on illustration margin
Title	32/32 Perpetua Bold
	Flush-left on text margin
Initial cap	50-point; typeface varies

Running heads

8-point New Baskerville Italic
One space between characters, three spaces between words

Folios

9-point Perpetua Bold
Verso: flush-left on illustration margin
Recto: flush-right on right text margin

Captions

9-point New Baskerville Italic

Index

A

Advertising copy   39
Aldus Manutius   110, 126
Alignment   30
    centered   35, 72, 195
    of columns   30
    flush-left/ragged-right   17, 27, 33, 72, 74, 196
    flush-right/ragged-left   17, 36, 196
    of headings   68-72
    justified   17, 30, 71
    of text   91
Announcements   65, 70, 129, 130
Art Nouveau   131
Ascender   42, 114, 146, 150, 195 (See also Descender; x-height.)
Asymmetry   34, 35, 173-175 (See also Balance.)

B

Balance   153
    in asymmetrical layouts   70, 173-175
    of black and white   12, 35, 75, 150, 157, 175
    of margins   33, 59, 69, 157, 174-175
Baskerville, John   52, 58, 120, 121, 181
Bauhaus   144
Benton, Morris   132
Bias (angle of stroke)   51, 149

Bindery   23, 183, 186
Bit-map   195
Blackletter   49, 90, 91, 128, 132, 195
Bodoni, Giambatista   53, 106, 122
Body copy   17, 18, 124 (See also Text.)
Boldface type   132, 195
    for contrast   63, 66
    as display   67, 69, 76, 99, 123
Book of Kells   129
Books
    dingbats   93
    margins   21, 31
    page design   63, 71
    paper   183
    typefaces   104, 105, 110, 112, 116, 118, 119, 126, 128, 129,
      132, 138, 142
    typography   49, 53, 58, 78
Borders   21, 23, 83, 94-99
Bowl   57, 149, 195 (See also Counter; Typeface architecture.)
Boxes   83, 94, 96
Budgeting resources   106, 184, 191-192
Business letters   8, 21, 52

C

Capital letters   150
    as display type   64, 72, 73-74, 88
    letter-spacing   40, 73
    line spacing of   67
    small   46, 64
Captions   63, 69
Catalogs   63, 132
Centering   195 (See also Alignment, centered.)
    display heads   34, 71, 75
    lines of type   71
    with ragged settings   34, 72
    tombstoning   71

Changes   12
    editorial   13
    last-minute   12, 189
    typographic   39, 80, 171
Chicago Manual of Style   13
Classifications
    of type   45-60, 103-152
Color   10, 66, 77, 114, 122, 124, 128, 144, 150
    in printing   179, 182, 183
    in typeface design   51, 53, 55
Columns   17, 21-22, 30, 34, 36, 66-72, 80, 172
Computer   179
    as aid to imagination   2, 89
    programs   13, 29, 65, 92, 95, 108
    replacing paper   13, 171
    and trial proofs   170-171
Conceptualization   168-172
Consistency   13, 17, 29, 82, 172
Contemporary typefaces   46, 57, 107, 140, 146
Content   8, 9, 12, 18, 56
Contrast   53, 63, 75, 76, 105
    in typeface design   51, 106, 149
Correspondence
    and type   28, 105, 110, 112
    on typewriters   28, 33
    on word processors   34
Counter   121, 149, 195 (See also Bowl.)

D

de Roos, S.H.   129
Decoration   76, 79, 87-100 (See also Dingbats; Initial Letters; Type.)
della Robbia, Luca   146
Descender   42, 110, 119, 146, 196 (See also Ascender; x-height.)
Design   155-160, 163-176 (See also Typeface design.)
    basic principles   7-12, 156-160
    consistency   24, 70, 82

continuity   10, 24, 156
and decoration   58, 87-100, 155
formal   34, 122
form and function   8, 71, 98, 165
harmony   157
informal   34, 53, 68, 69, 140
planning process   7-12, 156
purpose   9, 10, 155, 160
simplicity   158
Designers, professional   5, 87, 107, 132 (See also Expert help.)
Dingbats (Printers' flowers)   93, 100, 196
Display type   63-84, 115, 123, 124, 196
alignment   68-72
contrast in   66, 75-80
hierarchy in   80, 81
options   64-66, 89
size   80-82
spacing   66-67, 73-75
Doves Press   192
Drop caps   88, 89, 91-93, 196
Dummy   168, 169-70, 196
Duplicator service   179
Dutch type   47, 52, 55, 58, 106, 114, 126, 134

E

Editorial considerations   12-14, 164
Egyptian type   48, 54, 124
Elite type   27
Ellipses   41, 196
Ephemera (printed)   191
Expert help   179, 184
designers   5, 87, 107, 132, 184
illustrators   184
photographers   184
writers   167, 184

F

Families (See Typeface families.)
Figures   41, 42
    fractions   42
    lining   42
    old style   42
    in tabular work   42
Fitting (See Kerning.)
Flush-left (See Alignment.)
Flush-right (See Alignment.)
Flyers   70, 129
Folios   172, 196 (See also Page numbers.)
Font   46, 64-66, 107, 197 (See also Typeface.)
    contents of   46
    defined   44, 64, 197
    digital   41, 108, 180
    downloadable   180
    resident   104-105, 134-139, 180
    size   65
    "slurper"   104
Formal
    alignment   34, 71
    layout   34
    typeface design   110, 122, 134
Format   17-42, 167 (See also Size.)
    business letter   21
    newsletter   8
Franklin, Benjamin   118
Frutiger, Adrian   56
Fun   6, 193

G

Garamond, Claude   112
Gill, Eric   33, 56, 132, 142, 151
Goudy, Frederick W.   38, 128, 132

Grabhorn Press   132
Grabhorn, Robert   119
Graphic devices   94-100
    borders   94-97
    boxes   83, 94, 96
    graphic shapes   94
    rules   94
Grids   172-173, 197
    in layout design   172-173
    and sidebars   82-84
Griffo, Francesco   110
"Grotesque" type   124
Guides, column   27
Gutenberg, Johannes
    Bibles of   49, 184
    typefaces of   128

H

Hammer, Victor   129
Handwriting   94, 120, 126
    relation to type   2, 87, 90, 138
    styles   50, 51
Headlines   17, 63, 64, 65, 67-75, 77, 80-82
Helvetica   45, 56, 77, 80, 136-137
Hierarchies   158
House style   14 (See also Editorial considerations.)
Hyphenation   33, 197 (See also Justification.)
    adjusting   31, 32, 36
    programs   31, 36

I

Illustration   89, 95, 96, 98
Informal   34, 53, 68, 69, 140 (See also Formal.)
Initial letters   197 (See also Drop caps.)
    alignment of   88, 91-92
    history of   87

and printing   87-89, 91-93
    with small caps   92
Ink   51, 179, 181, 183
Italic type   48, 64, 110, 126-127
    defined   126, 197
    as display   64-65, 120
    with pull-quotes   82, 83

J

Johnston, Edward   142
Justification   30-33
    adjustments to   32
    and hyphenation   31-33, 36-37
    and "rivers"   31

K

Kerning   40, 197 (See also Letter spacing.)
    manually   74
    pairs   38, 73
    and tracking   36
Keyboarding   13
Kis, Nikolas   114, 126, 140

L

Laser printers (See Printers, laser.)
Layout   6, 7, 17-42, 79, 163-176, 197
    organic   173-175, 198
    using a grid   172-173
Leading   197
    and alignment   29-30
    and display type   66-67
    and line length   26, 114
    and type size   30
Leaves   170
Legibility

of display type   75

with line length   28

Letter spacing   38-40 (See also Kerning; Tracking.)

of capitals   40, 73

defined   194

and line length   72

manual   74

Line length   26, 28

Line space   29-30 (See also Leading.)

Lowercase   38, 49, 88, 150

Livre de luxe   122

M

Magazines   112

Manuscript   168

decorative initials in   87

electronic   13-14

Margin   18-25, 30-36, 59, 68-71, 97, 157, 173-175, 198 (See also White space.)

alignment   24, 30-36

ragged   27, 31, 33, 36, 99, 174

size   19

Markup   13

Meidinger, Max   56, 136

Minuscule alphabet   49

Modern type   52-53, 198

Money   191-192 (See also Budgeting resources.)

Morison, Stanley   114, 134

N

Newsletters

design   8-10

pull-quotes and sidebars   82-84

typefaces   110, 115, 119, 123, 138

typography   66, 78

O

Old Style type   50-52, 55, 105, 106, 198

P

Page layout programs   12-13, 29, 38, 40, 80, 168-169, 180
Page numbers   172 (See also Folios.)
Paper   184-188
    conservation   187
    recycling   187
    types and grades of   180, 181, 185-186
Photocopy service   181
Photographers   184
Photographs   181
    halftone   182, 184
Phototypesetting   138
Pica   27, 198
Point   27, 39, 198
"Pouring" text   13, 36
Printer   199
    ink-jet   186
    laser   146, 181, 182, 185
    offset   181, 182
    resolution   181, 182
    system file (resident fonts)   104-105, 180
Printers' flowers (See Dingbats.)
Printing firms   182-183
Production   10, 179-188
    assistance   182-184
    tools   179-181
Proportional type   27
Pull-quotes   82-84, 199
Punctuation   41

Q

Quotation marks   41

R

Ragged margin (See Margin.)
Renaissance type   50, 58
Renner, Paul   144
Resident fonts (See Font, resident.)
Resolution   199
    of printers   181, 182
    and typefaces   109
Reverses   89, 99, 199
    typefaces for   99
Revival type designs   55
Rivers   31, 37 (See also White space.)
Rogers, Bruce   58
Runarounds   98

S

Sans-serif   56
    defined   48, 199
    emergence of   56
    typefaces   142-147
Screen tints   95
Script type   90, 91, 130, 199
Serif type   47-48
    defined   47, 199
    Modern   48, 52-53, 122
    Old Style   48, 50-52, 55
    shapes   48, 148
    slab   48, 54
    Transitional   48, 52, 122
Service bureau   103, 108, 182
Set-width   199
Sidebar   82-84, 200

Size   166-167, 169 (See also Format; Type size.)

Slimbach, Robert   105

Small capitals   46, 200

    with initial letters   92

Software

    page layout   38, 80, 168-169, 180

    sources for   207

Space (See White space.)

Special characters   93-94, 100 (See also Dingbats.)

    bullets   100

    ligatures   100

Special effects   131

    with illustration programs   89

Squinting   12, 71

Steel-pen lettering   130

Stem   57, 200

    contrast   57, 149

    modeling   150

Stone, Sumner   107, 140

Strokes

    angle of   51, 149

    horizontal   148

    oblique   51

    pen   51, 130

    vertical   150

Structure   9-10

    continuity   156-157

    logical flow   10, 82

Subheads   66, 67, 81

Suppliers

    of printing services   182-183

    of type   107-109, 207

Sutcliffe, Judith   132

Swiss type   47 (See also Helvetica.)

Symmetry   71 (See also Asymmetry.)

T

Tail   151

Tailpiece   94

Tarr, John C.   57

Text   17, 63, 163 (See also Body copy.)

    file   13

    setting   13, 56

Thin space   32, 73

Thumbnail sketch   168-169, 200

Title pages   78

Tombstoning   71

    spacing   72

    with ragged settings   72

Tools   179-181

Tracking   38-40

    adjusting   39

    defined   38, 200

    and letter combinations   39-40

Transitional type   52, 106, 200

Trial proofs   170-172

    on computer screen   170

Tschichold, Jan   35

Type

    defined   2, 200

    designers   46, 108, 132

    digital   109

    display   63-84

    history of   49-58, 106

    makers (suppliers)   107-109, 207

    manipulation of   70, 89, 108, 171

    as ornamentation   87-100

    size   27-28, 29, 30, 65, 80-82, 119, 200

    special effects with   89, 95

    weight   149, 151

Type combinations   75-80, 93, 105

    rules of thumb   76-80

    unconventional   80

Typeface   2, 45-60, 103-152, 201
    architecture   148-152
    classifications   49, 109-147
    color   10, 53, 55, 151
    combinations   64, 76-80, 105, 106
    design   4, 46, 124
    families   5, 46, 140
    personality of   4, 57, 58, 60, 79, 106, 150
    variants   5, 28, 49
    versions   107-109
Typesetting   13, 27-29
Typewriter
    letter spacing   27
    type sizes   27
    vs. word processors   28
Typography   45-60, 103-152
    allusive   58, 60
    basic principles of   156-160
    consistency in   159-160
    defined   3, 201
    logical flow in   156-157
    simplicity in   158

U

Uncial   129, 201
Updike, Daniel Berkeley   49
Uppercase   48-49, 64

W

Weight (See Type, weight.)
"Western" typefaces   54
White space (See also Alignment; Letter spacing; Word spacing.)
    and columns   22, 71
    dynamics of   5, 10-12, 25, 68, 69, 92
    in margins   18-19
    and symmetry   66-67, 72

"rivers"   31, 37
Wilson, Adrian   78, 129
Woodcut type   90, 91, 131
Word processing   13
    relation to typography   12, 41
    text string   13
Word spacing   36, 37, 73 (See also Alignment.)
Writers   13, 164, 184

X

x-height   114, 140, 201

Z

Zapf, Hermann   4, 56, 106, 132, 138, 146

the
Ventana Press

Desktop Design Series

The Presentation Design Book

$24.95
280 pages, Illustrated
ISBN: 0-940087-37-5

How to design effective, attractive slides, overheads, graphs, diagrams, handouts and screen shows with your desktop computer.

Newsletters from the Desktop

$23.95
290 pages, Illustrated
ISBN: 0-940087-40-5

Now the millions of desktop publishers who produce newsletters can learn how to improve the design of their publications.

The Makeover Book: 101 Design Solutions for Desktop Publishing

$17.95
245 pages, Illustrated
ISBN: 0-940087-20-0

"Before-and-after" desktop publishing examples demonstrate how basic design revisions can dramatically improve a document.

Looking Good in Print

(100,000 in print!)
$23.95
230 pages, Illustrated
ISBN: 0-940087-05-7

The most widely used reference book for desktop design offers dozens of tips and tricks that help you add style and appeal to your documents. For use with any hardware and software.

Desktop Publishing with WordPerfect

$21.95
350 pages, Illustrated
ISBN: 0-940087-15-4

WordPerfect offers graphics capabilities that can save users thousands of dollars in design and typesetting costs. Includes invaluable information on creating style sheets for consistency and speed.

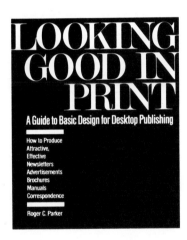

TO ORDER additional copies of *Type from the Desktop,* or any of the other books in our desktop design series, please fill out this order form and return it to us for quick shipment.

	Quantity		Price		Total
Type from the Desktop	_____	x	$23.95	=	$_____
The Presentation Design Book	_____	x	$23.95	=	$_____
Newsletters from the Desktop	_____	x	$23.95	=	$_____
Looking Good in Print	_____	x	$23.95	=	$_____
Desktop Publishing w/ WordPerfect	_____	x	$21.95	=	$_____
The Makeover Book	_____	x	$17.95	=	$_____

Shipping: Please add $3.60/first book for standard UPS, $1.35/book thereafter;
$6/book UPS "two-day air," $1.35/book thereafter.
For Canada, add $5.35/book.   = $_____

Send C.O.D. (add $3.30 to shipping charges)   = $_____

North Carolina residents add 5% sales tax   = $_____

Total   = $_____

Name _____

Company _____

Address (No P.O. Box) _____

City _____ State _____ Zip _____

Daytime Phone _____

_____ Payment enclosed (check or money order; no cash please)

____ VISA   ____ MC   Acc't # _____ - _____ - _____ - _____

Expiration date _____   Signature _____

Please mail or fax to:

Ventana Press, P.O. Box 2468, Chapel Hill, NC 27515

919/942-0220, FAX: 919/942-1140.

TO ORDER additional copies of *Type from the Desktop*, or any of the other books in our desktop design series, please fill out this order form and return it to us for quick shipment.

	Quantity		Price		Total
Type from the Desktop	_____	x	$23.95	=	$_____
The Presentation Design Book	_____	x	$23.95	=	$_____
Newsletters from the Desktop	_____	x	$23.95	=	$_____
Looking Good in Print	_____	x	$23.95	=	$_____
Desktop Publishing w/ WordPerfect	_____	x	$21.95	=	$_____
The Makeover Book	_____	x	$17.95	=	$_____

Shipping: Please add $3.60/first book for standard UPS, $1.35/book thereafter; $6/book UPS "two-day air," $1.35/book thereafter. For Canada, add $5.35/book.   = $_____

Send C.O.D. (add $3.30 to shipping charges)   = $_____

North Carolina residents add 5% sales tax   = $_____

                                                                  Total   = $_____

Name _____

Company _____

Address (No P.O. Box) _____

City _____ State _____ Zip _____

Daytime Phone _____

_____ Payment enclosed (check or money order; no cash please)

____ VISA   ____ MC   Acc't # _____ - _____ - _____ - _____

Expiration date _____   Signature _____

Please mail or fax to:

Ventana Press, P.O. Box 2468, Chapel Hill, NC 27515

919/942-0220, FAX: 919/942-1140.

TO ORDER additional copies of *Type from the Desktop*, or any of the other books in our desktop design series, please fill out this order form and return it to us for quick shipment.

	Quantity	Price	Total
Type from the Desktop	_____ x	$23.95 =	$_____
The Presentation Design Book	_____ x	$23.95 =	$_____
Newsletters from the Desktop	_____ x	$23.95 =	$_____
Looking Good in Print	_____ x	$23.95 =	$_____
Desktop Publishing w/ WordPerfect	_____ x	$21.95 =	$_____
The Makeover Book	_____ x	$17.95 =	$_____

Shipping: Please add $3.60/first book for standard UPS, $1.35/book thereafter; $6/book UPS "two-day air," $1.35/book thereafter. For Canada, add $5.35/book.   = $_____

Send C.O.D. (add $3.30 to shipping charges)   = $_____

North Carolina residents add 5% sales tax   = $_____

Total   = $_____

Name _____

Company _____

Address (No P.O. Box) _____

City _____ State _____ Zip _____

Daytime Phone _____

_____ Payment enclosed (check or money order; no cash please)

____ VISA   ____ MC   Acc't # _____ - _____ - _____ - _____

Expiration date _____   Signature _____

Please mail or fax to:

Ventana Press, P.O. Box 2468, Chapel Hill, NC 27515

919/942-0220, FAX: 919/942-1140.